Howard Hughes

The Pocket Essential

AMERICAN INDIAN WARS

D0530786

www.pocketessentials.com

First published in Great Britain 2001 by Pocket Essentials, 18 Coleswood Road, Harpenden, Herts, AL5 1EQ

Distributed in the USA by Trafalgar Square Publishing, PO Box 257, Howe Hill Road, North Pomfret, Vermont 05053

A CIP catalogue record for this book is available from the British Library.

ISBN 1-903047-73-0

2 4 6 8 10 9 7 5 3 1

Book typeset by Pdunk
Printed and bound by Cox & Wyman

for Mum and Dad

Acknowledgements

Thanks to Nick Rennison, Paul Duncan (for valuable source material), Alex Coe (extra research and material), Glynne Welby (Civil War material), Mike Coppack (Indian Wars material), Isabel, Rhian, Belinda, Chris, Ion, Mike Oaks and especially to Clara.

CONTENTS

Death On The Plains:
An Introduction To The Indian Wars

The story of the American Wild West is a conflicting mixture of half-remembered facts and make believe. In the public's perception, the West is largely a myth. Through TV, pulp novels, art and cinema, the West has been presented in wildly differing forms, from a place of romance, optimism and valour, to a morass of violence, corruption and lies. As far as the original inhabitants of the West were concerned, it was the second that was closer to the truth. This was the West of history books, a wild, inhospitable, unforgiving land that harboured danger at every turn, in sharp contrast to the idealised views Easterners often had of it. Easterners thought the West was free range, a 'Garden of Eden', just waiting to be colonised. Views soon changed however and the pioneers' adventures out West could become, quite literally, hair-raising.

An American Dream

At the beginning of the 1840s the North American Indians looked across the plains at the unstoppable expansion of the white man's West. It seemed inconceivable that a land that was theirs by birthright could be taken away from them. During the following decades of conflict, as the settlers pushed onward through the 'Virgin Land' (which wasn't virgin at all), the Indians saw their way of life disappear before their eyes. For the next 40 years they desperately clung to a dream, the terrible consequences of which left the once proud Indians reduced to living in appalling conditions on reservations. It was certainly true that danger haunted the settlers every step of the way. After setting off in covered wagons and coasting through lush grasslands, pioneers were often alarmed when hostile Indians ran off their horses in the night. If the settlers were lucky enough to arrive at their destination, knock-together a makeshift cabin and set up home, their tranquillity could be broken in a moment. While away hunting, a husband could return to find his hard toil and loved ones gone forever. His house burned, his wife murdered and scalped (or worse captured) and his prized stock run-off. Such was the ferocity of an Indian attack. But was killing every Indian in sight really the solution?

The extreme danger posed by Indians was in addition to the other perils of frontier life, among them drought, starvation, disease and the weather. In one instance a wagon train was wiped out, not by an Indian attack, but when these natural perils coincided with horrific results. In August 1846, the inexperienced 'Donner Party' (a group of settlers heading to the Californian gold fields from Fort Bridger) made the fateful decision to take an alleged shortcut, called the 'Hastings Cut-off.' As it was, the 'Cut-off' turned out to be aptly named, though not because it reduced the distance to California. The party became trapped in a particularly terrible winter. Snowbound, they began to starve and eventually resorted to cannibalism. Of the 88 settlers who had set out, only 49 survived - the relief party couldn't reach them until February 1847. But of all these perils, it was the Indians who proved most problematic to the whites. When the settlers started to complain about the harassing Indian attacks on what they believed to be 'their' land, the army got involved. However, the Indians had a very good argument in favour of their ownership of the land - they were there first. Not only that, they had been there a very long time.

Land Of My Fathers

The first visitors to America were Vikings, who landed in 1000AD, but it was formally discovered nearly 500 years later by Christopher Columbus, who claimed it for the King of Spain. These first European arrivals called the red-skinned, feather-wearing natives 'Indios' when they landed in 1492. English-speaking settlers arrived in 1607, building the first settlement at Jamestown. The Indians the European settlers found on the east coast were made up of many tribes. Some were hunter-gatherers, others had adopted primitive farming methods. The mistake made by the Europeans was not an unusual one for people encountering a new race for the first time. Because the Indians couldn't speak a European language, they were uncultured savages, living in primitive conditions and crying out to be taught European ways and customs. The Indians got along well with their new neighbours initially, but as immigrants arrived by the boatload, and the settlers started to move inland, the Indians turned on the whites. These eastern Indians were pacified (or just plain decimated) in a series of bloody wars with the settlers. The first was the Pequot War of 1636 (which ended in an Indian defeat) and the major fracas of the period was King Philip's War of 1675-78. Philip (whose Indian name was Metacomet) was accused of plotting against the settlers. The lengthy conflict was defined by a series of attacks on towns and prolonged sieges, which again ended in the Indians' capitulation (and Philip's death).

These early wars set the pattern for the later, more familiar, Indian Wars. Usually a minor incident caused the peace to be broken, followed by a large-scale raid (invariably resulting in a massacre). Then the rebellion would be quelled by the army, with each side blaming the other for starting the conflict. Over the next two hundred years, the Indians were gradually shunted inland and squashed between areas of white settlement. Both the British and the 'Americans' (as the settlers came to be known) used Indians in the War of Independence (1775-83), though the Indians initially tried not to get involved. They were also allied to forces during the French and Indian Wars that broke out intermittently between 1689 and 1763 (the so-called 'Trapper Wars') and the War of 1812. But by the early 1800's nearly all the eastern Indians had been pushed into 'designated areas' or had been driven further inland. In the late 18th and early 19th Century, Europe lost interest in American affairs and both Spain and France pulled out of North America. At this stage, the bulk of North America, from the west coast to the Mississippi, was uncharted and full of Indians. In 1803, in the so-called Louisiana Purchase, the Americans bought 800,000 square miles of land beyond the Mississippi River from the French for the modest sum of $15,000,000. This now meant that America owned most of the land westward from the Mississippi. There was one problem - the colonists about to settle the land would have to get rid of the current occupants.

An Unhappy Chapter

It was the Californian Gold Rush of 1849 that began the westward push which resulted in the most famous Indian Wars. Many hundreds of thousands of Indians had already been killed by diseases brought by the whitemen. This latest influx of whites eager to get-rich-quick meant the Indians had to do something to protect their homeland. Soon afterwards, the Indians began hostilities and started to attack the intruders. The government countered this with a huge treaty in 1851. Dubbed the Treaty of Laramie, this involved a massive gathering of Northern Indians at Fort Laramie, the largest council ever assembled. The government offered to pay the Indians $50,000 a year plus guns (for hunting purposes, of course) if they stopped attacking the Forty-niners' wagons. Another provision was that the Indians must stay in their own 'designated areas' (in the days before they were called reservations), a concept completely alien to the free-roaming, nomadic Indians' lifestyle. In retrospect, getting the Indians to comply was like trying to tell fish to stay in their own part of the ocean. Indians knew no borders, only rough tribal territorial boundaries. Moreover, these tribal boundaries were there to be broken - the acquisition of hunting land was one of the main reasons for inter-tribal conflict. But for a complete outsider like the white man to arrive and steal the land was something the Indians wouldn't stand for. The Indians had a great deal of trouble understanding many of the white man's ideas. They never fathomed the value of money and were uncomprehending of the white man's lust for the 'yellow metal' found in abundance in the hills. They also had trouble with the notion of countrywide government. For instance, Geronimo thought that each group of troops sent after him represented a local town, rather than any larger governmental department. Therefore, with this reasoning, he thought that each town had its own little army to defend it, without realising the wider picture.

In 1853 the Southern tribes signed a similar treaty to the Laramie deal, protecting the Santa Fe Trail trading route. But thereafter, the government didn't look after the 'pacified' Indians very well. Poor supplies and exploitation resulted in starvation and disease. Moreover the uneasy peace resulted in more troops arriving to police the frontier should trouble begin. In this atmosphere of disquiet, trouble was never far away. In August 1854, near Fort Laramie, an argument over an injured cow resulted in the first real action of the post-Laramie Treaty Indian Wars. The Indians accused of injuring the animal were Sioux and the army got involved. A 30-man army contingent was sent to catch the culprits in a nearby village. The inexperienced lieutenant in charge, itching for a fight, lost his patience and opened fire on the village. The Indians went berserk and slaughtered the command to a man. Nearly a year later, in August 1855, the army sought retribution for the outrage and 600 soldiers levelled the Indian village on Ash Creek, the site of the previous massacre. It was the first instance of the US Army marching straight to the source of the trouble and stemming it at grassroots level. Their victims included women and children. But the 'Indian Troubles', as they were vaguely referred to, were interrupted by the small matter of the American Civil War.

Many Indians saw the War as an opportunity to get their land back. The settlers were largely defenceless, with most of the troops away in the east, and the Indian fighting during the Civil War was amongst the bloodiest of the conflict. Settlers were murdered, while the Indians' only opponents were poorly armed but vicious militiamen. These violent squabbles reached their zenith in the Civil War years, with the Minnesota Massacre (an Indian atrocity) and the Sand Creek Massacre (perpetrated by the army). In the first, the Santee Sioux, dissatisfied with their lifestyle under white supervision, ran riot throughout Minnesota in 1862, sacking towns and killing indiscriminately. In the second, the Colorado Volunteers, dissatisfied that they had been recruited but hadn't shot any Indians, ran riot in 1864, in retribution for the Minnesota Massacre, attacking a peaceful Cheyenne village and killing indiscriminately. In 1866, Captain Fetterman's command was wiped out by the Sioux and Cheyenne during Red Cloud's War, in retribution for the Sand Creek massacre…a pattern was emerging.

The Vanishing American

The Sand Creek Massacre was one of the darkest events in American history. Colonel Chivington, the Volunteers' commander was a racist ex-preacher who harboured political ambitions. Seeking fame, he deliberately stirred up trouble between the whites and the Indians, providing him with the excuse to attack the peaceful camp of Black Kettle. The whole affair, which involved the soldiers slaughtering many Indian women and children, had startling parallels with the uncontrollable carnage of the My Lai massacre in the Vietnam War, over a century later. The episodes in Minnesota and Sand Creek began the Plains Wars in earnest and defined the ferocity with which they would be fought. No one would be safe in this horrific war of attrition. Many of the most famous Indians warriors and chiefs made their names during the early, post-Civil War period, leading gallant forays against the whites. Similarly, officers who had fought well in the Civil War, were despatched West to distinguish themselves (or otherwise) against the Indians. But the Indians were a very different enemy to the Confederates the officers had had to face back east. Most soldiers were eager for a crack at the 'savages', but they were most surprised to find the Indians a formidable foe, who made maximum use of the only tactic in their repertoire - the ambush.

In 1866, following the Civil War, the army decided to concentrate their efforts on subduing the Indians across the West. Many of the conflicts and antagonisms that flared into full-scale wars were age-old squabbles. For example, in the Southwest, the Apaches hated the local Hispanics, the Hispanics hated the Indians and the whites wanted to rid the territory of both groups. The 'Indian Problem' here wasn't that they were attacking farms and wagon trains, but the simple reason that they were free to roam as they pleased - it was a war of territory. Conflicts elsewhere resulted from the Indians harassing wagon trains heading West along trails which was an obvious breach of treaties previously negotiated with the Indians. In 1866, the government dispatched the US Army to protect one such route - the Bozeman Trail, through Wyoming and Montana - by constructing a trio of forts. But the plan ended in disaster as a consequence of concentrated resistance in the area, led by Sioux chief Red Cloud. Firstly a detachment of 80 men under the foolhardy leadership of Captain Fetterman was massacred, then the forts were besieged and the army was eventually forced to abandon the plan (and the stockades) the following year.

Meanwhile in Texas and New Mexico, the Comanches and Kiowas waged the War of the Staked Plains against the soldiers. The Comanches were led by Chief Quanah, who was half white and who later took his mother's English surname Parker, when he ended up living on a reservation. The discovery of gold in the Black Hills of Dakota in 1874 by an expeditionary force led by Custer resulted in a further outbreak of hostilities in Dakota and Montana, as prospectors flocked to the hills that the Indians held sacred. This resulted in the most famous Indian War of them all, the Sioux War of 1875-76. A massive three-column army campaign was mounted against the Indians, who had banded together to form a super-force, with the Sioux chief Sitting Bull at their head. But things went tragically awry for the army. Initially, one column under General Crook was halted at the Battle of the Rosebud and then Custer wilfully disobeyed orders to wait for the fractured offensive to converge on the Indians in the Big Horn region of Montana. He attacked the massive force of Indians with only five companies of the 7th Cavalry (about 215 men). His whole command was annihilated in the catastrophic action known ever since as 'Custer's Last Stand.' The following year the Sioux and Cheyenne were crushed decisively by another sustained offensive. Crazy Horse was killed, while Sitting Bull fled into exile in Canada.

To the west of Montana another drama was unfolding. Chief Joseph led his tribe, the Nez Perce, away from their homeland and toward the sanctuary of the Canadian border. This epic 108-day journey concluded with the Indians being stopped before reaching the border, having travelled 1700 miles. It was at this point that Chief Joseph, a great orator, delivered the most moving speech ever heard on the plains, which concluded, "From where the sun now stands, I will fight no more forever." To the south, in the blazing deserts of Texas, Arizona and New Mexico the Apaches had been fighting the Mexicans and Americans for decades. Their ferocious guerrilla tactics meant that they earned a reputation as the army's most formidable opponents. In celebrated engagements like the Battle of Apache Pass the names of their chiefs - Mangas Coloradas, Cochise and Victorio - became famous. But by the 1870's the Apaches' fight was drawing to a close, with many of their bravest leaders dead. Only holdouts like Geronimo would continue to lead the army a merry dance well into the next decade.

Fighting Fire With Fire

The Indian Wars were a peculiar period for the US Army, and one they're not especially proud of. For many years little was made of their final victory over the Indians, because of the shameful nature of that victory. For example, study texts used by American military academies in the sixties had scant regard for the Indian Wars (which are invariably described as 'ugly'). One such text devoted over 60 pages to the Civil War, with much discussion of tactics (backed-up by complicated diagrams) and comparisons with similar strategic developments in Europe. The Indian Wars warranted 9 pages (in the self-explanatory chapter entitled 'The Dark Ages Of The US Army 1865-98'), a single map and a rather depressing photo of grave markers on Custer's Hill. What cadets could learn from this is anyone's guess, the consensus being that there weren't really any tactics in the Indian Wars. The chapter concluded appropriately. It stated that the soldiers who fought in these campaigns did so under the most extreme of circumstances, 'Yet through perseverance and a strong sense of obligation to duty, the army saw its task through to successful completion.'

Much has been made of the hardships of Indian campaigning. The discomfort suffered by the troops out West was particularly difficult to deal with. On many forays, morale was low and desertion rife. The living conditions for enlisted men in the far-flung frontier forts were often appalling, although officers' quarters were sometimes more luxurious. There was also the terrible boredom. But due to the inhospitable topography, the weather and the Indians, life on the campaign trail was much worse than in the barracks, though seldom as boring. The summer campaigns were terrible due to the blistering heat, dusty trails (which enveloped the soldiers in great clouds and turned their uniforms from blue to powdery grey) and a complete dependency on a reliable water supply. The winter was no better, with the onset of blizzards, snowdrifts, extreme cold and a complete dependency on a reliable compass. Between the two seasons, there were several other conditions to look forward to, including rain, fog and mud. If an army commander mistimed an offensive, he could easily get bogged down, like General Crook's 1876 campaign, which began in the autumn sunshine but soon sank in a sea of mud. One of the big problems for the US Army on the march in hostile country was the supply lines. Wagons always slowed down an offensive and mule trains weren't much better. They were also sitting targets for the Indians, who quickly caught on to the idea that an army marched on its stomach. But following the comparative failure of several campaigns, the army did learn from their mistakes and came up with some really innovative tactics. These included using smaller flying columns (who travelled light, to keep up with the hostiles), exploiting advances in communication (including the heliograph, especially useful against the Apache) and a more tenacious attitude to winter campaigning. This last aspect was pioneered by Colonel Miles, who wrapped his infantry in Buffalo coats, furry mittens and muskrat hats. He was never a quitter and his victories against the Indians in the harshness of midwinter earned him the nickname 'Bearcoat Miles.'

But campaigning at any time of year didn't really suit the troops. The terrain was treacherous and there was the constant threat of being bush-whacked. It was a wise commander who could spot an ambush. Some of the worst campaigns were the consequence of inept leadership. Some commanders, like Major Reno and General Crook, were criticised for being too timid. Others were far too reckless for their own good, though sometimes their recklessness paid off. Gamblers like Custer at Washita River and Forsyth at Beecher's Island were lucky to get way with their lives, when they bit off more than they could chew. On other occasions this wilfulness spelt the end. Prime examples include Custer, this time at the Little Big Horn (where his proverbial luck ran out) and Captain Fetterman, who met his match in Crazy Horse, during Red Cloud's War. The Indian Wars were a learning curve for the army, but it certainly wasn't the 'tactic-less' affair that many commentators imply.

No matter how long soldiers spent out West, they had to remember every lesson they learned - it was essential for survival. Lesson number one was: 'Don't follow the decoys.' It was a lesson that took an awfully long time to sink in. Time after time, a command of soldiers blindly followed a small group of Indians into a huge trap. The soldiers' second lesson was that the Indians were masters at the art of camouflage. The most innocuous looking thicket could harbour a war party, while a broken, pockmarked landscape could conceal an army of hundreds. Such immense ambushes could result in the massacre of entire commands, with the Indians rising out of the ground at the soldiers' feet. An irony was that at some points in the Indian Wars, the Indians had better firearms than the army. This was highlighted at Custer's Last Stand, where the cavalry had old-style carbines (which were prone to jamming if they were fired incessantly), while many of the Indians had Winchester repeaters - traded or stolen throughout the spring of 1876.

Once they had made their presence known, the Indians charged - shrieking and whooping, to put the fear of God into the soldiers. They were covered with feathers and paint, and waved war lances and tomahawks. At the first opportunity they would close in for hand-to-hand fighting. Any soldier who faced such a terrible onslaught would never forget it. The Indians only had this one tactic - and a slight variation on it, whereby they would approach a wagon train pretending to be friendly, before slaughtering the settlers where they stood. It was very rare for the Indians and the whites to square up for a battle with anything remotely resembling conventional tactics. So in the late 1860's, the army, realising that fighting the Indians in the summer wasn't working, began to fight in the winter. They also adapted their methods of fighting, abandoning the big columns and instead using smaller groups of very experienced Indian fighters. The idea was to draw the Indians out, by persuading them that the small group of soldiers consisted of raw recruits. But after the Forsyth debacle at Beecher's Island (where one such force was besieged on an island for over a week), the army returned to their original strategy. The army later employed scouts, either recruited from members of the tribe they were fighting (who had already been defeated) or from their tribal enemies, who were always keen to lend a hand. It eventually became clear that to catch an Indian, you must also learn how to think like one.

What Name You Called?

It is the personalities and names of the protagonists that have perpetu- ated the mystique of the American West. The great battles of the Indian Wars are always presented as a clash of titans - Custer against Sitting Bull or Crook versus Geronimo. It was these personalities that always lived on after the actual events. The image of Custer, dressed in buckskins, with flowing blond hair and waving a sabre, riding into the valley of death is a potent one, though inaccurate on most counts. Custer wasn't wearing buck- skins at the Little Big Horn, had his hair cut short and wasn't carrying a sabre. Few army commanders of the period were as romanticised - only Forsyth (after Beecher's Island), Crook (for his dogged pursuit of the Apache) and Miles (for his dogged pursuit of just about everybody) came close. Other marginal figures were also feted as Indian fighters, including individualists like Buffalo Bill Cody.

The Indian Wars were also hugely inspirational to artists of the time and their depiction of various key events colours our perception of the conflict. Painters like Charles Schreyvogel, Edgar Paxson, Fredric Remington, Otto Becker and Robert Lindneux perfectly captured the excitement, terror, pathos and horror of frontier warfare, with their version of events, like the Sand Creek and Washita Massacres, Beecher's Island and Custer's Last Stand. Most were based on years of research - Schreyvogel for instance had never witnessed a real battle. Most artistic impressions of the actual Last Stand, with Custer standing among the piles of corpses as one of the last soldiers to be killed, are open to conjecture. Some battle site accounts report finding his body nowhere near the Last Stand site, but in a position that implied he died a lot earlier in the engagement. Similarly, many of the Indians became impressive historical figures, but their own retrospective storytelling embellished the truth. Their world *was* a world of myths, mys- ticism and magic, and the accounts of their warriors' exploits often read like passages from Greek mythology. They also had wonderfully evocative names. Names that epitomised the men they described - Crazy Horse, Crow Killer or Hawk That Hunts Walking. These Indian names usually had interesting stories behind them. They include Apache chief Mangas Coloradas (which translates as 'Red Sleeves' because he wore a red shirt in battle), Nez Perce Chief Joseph (because he was baptised with a Christian name), the warrior Geronimo (from a Mexican battle cry to Saint Jerome) and the Comanche prophet Coyote Droppings (perhaps best not to ask).

But there is a very clear link between the Indian myth-making and its white equivalent. In the same way that Indian warriors would recount their exploits in battle (to their comrades and family around the campfire), so too would the Indian fighters, similarly embroidering the truth. This way, relatively little-known men - like the gallant defenders of Adobe Walls (a sort of Comanche Rorke's Drift) - became heroes to every white on the frontier. Literature helped this romanticism, with everyone from dime novel hacks to Longfellow contributing to the mythology. Enhancing this mythology were the usual attention-seeking cranks, saying ridiculous things like they survived the Fetterman or Custer massacres, or they shot Crazy Horse. Moreover, in the same way gunfighters upped their number of duels and victories, so battle casualties in the Indian Wars (as reported by both sides) are notoriously inaccurate. The army always played down their losses, while the Indians invariably removed all trace of their dead from the battlefield, for ceremonial burial later. But the events of the Indian Wars were impressive enough without further exaggeration. Among the outrageous acts of heroism, one instantly thinks of Portugee Phillips and his mercy dash through blizzards and Indian patrols, to break Red Cloud's siege on the Bozeman forts in 1866. Phillips was like the hero of a melodrama, but every part of his amazing journey (right down to his arrival at his destination during the Christmas Eve ball) is true.

Little Big Wars

There were many Indian Wars that hardly merit a mention in the history books and then only as a footnote to some other, more important, event. Two such events were the Modoc War of 1872-73 and the government's unsubtle handling of the Navajos in the 1860's. The biggest of these little wars, certainly as far as the press coverage goes, was the Modoc War. The Modocs lived in California in an inhospitable area known as the Lava Beds, also called the 'Land of Burnt Out Fires', so called because of the volcanic activity in the area. In 1872 a genius in the government decided to put the Modocs on a reservation with their sworn enemies, the Klamath. Neither party was particularly happy with this arrangement and the

Modocs, who were in the minority, left the site and returned to their homeland. In November 1872, the army arrived to put the Modocs back on their reservation. But fighting broke out and the Modocs' leader, Kientpoos, known by the English epithet 'Captain Jack' (because he wore a US Army jacket) went on the run with about 160 men, women and children. They hid out in the lava beds and managed to repulse even the most sustained army assaults. The deadlock lasted throughout the winter and on into spring. The lava beds offered ideal cover for the Modocs, who put up a stalwart defence. Eventually they agreed to meet the army halfway and attended a peace talk on Good Friday, 1873. But during the powwow, Captain Jack shot the army's commander, General Canby at point blank range. Not only was the peace talk over, so was any chance of leniency from the army. Now a massive force was assembled to hunt the Modocs through the lava beds. By June, lack of supplies forced Captain Jack to give up, but Canby's cold-blooded assassination ensured he swung from the gallows. During his adventures in the lava beds, Captain Jack became something of folk hero to the American people, an opinion that changed after the little folk hero shot their general through the head. Canby remains the only general ever to have died during the Indian Wars.

The once-proud Navajo tribe had an even worse time of it. The Navajos lived in New Mexico and Arizona. In the early years of the Civil War, while the whites fought each other, the Navajo's began to attack local settlements. The army retaliated without remorse, determined to bring the Navajos to the reservation at Bosque Redondo, which was basically a desolate salt flat. Kit Carson, the celebrated Indian fighter, who had already herded the Mascalero Apaches into custody, was put in charge of the operation. In June 1863 the 1st Cavalry New Mexico Volunteers, under Carson, countered these 'hostiles' (many of whom were innocent and were happy living where they were) by burning their crops. Consequently the Indians starved. The campaign was a brutal affair and not particularly successful until Carson attacked the heart of the Navajos' homeland, the Cañon de Chelly, in November. It had a reputation as an impregnable, fortress-like stronghold. But the Navajos Carson found there were in no fit state to fight. The 8000 captives Carson took were marched 300 miles to Bosque Redondo and died in droves on the way. The Indians called the sorry march the 'Long Walk.' In the following months, there was no longer a 'Navajo Problem', nor indeed very much of a tribe, though they did recover from their atrocious treatment and returned to live in peace in their homeland in 1868.

The Last Dance

By the late 1880's, with the Indian Nations effectively defeated, the Sioux and Cheyenne briefly rose again, with the insurgence of the Ghost Dance Cult. The cult spread rapidly through the despondent ranks of reservation Indians, who were desperate for something to believe in. The Ghost Dance, a shuffling, trance-inducing endurance test, promised the Indians there would be a return to the old days. But the army was worried. Even though the doctrine preached pacifism, the medicine could be powerful enough to cause the Indians to rise up against the troops. When Sitting Bull became a disciple he was arrested by the Indian Police, but in a scuffle was shot in the back and killed. Other Sioux, under Chief Big Foot, feared reprisals and fled the reservation. But they were captured by the army at Wounded Knee Creek. During the surrender, trouble started and the troops lashed the Sioux with cannon fire. It was one of the worst (but thankfully the last) massacres of the Indian Wars.

With the death of Sitting Bull and the Battle of Wounded Knee (both 1890), the Indian Wars drew to an ignominious conclusion. The Ghost Dance was their last hurrah. Finally the 'savages' were pacified and the West was a safe place for white folks. But reservation life took a terrible toll on the Indians, decimating their numbers and forcing them to inhabit a land that was unfamiliar and embrace a lifestyle that was alien. Present day Indian reservations bear little resemblance to those of their ancestors. For instance, descendants of the famous Mohawk tribe live on a reservation in Connecticut, where they run a casino. Elsewhere, the quaint huddle of tepees, squaws making moccasins and brightly coloured totem poles are strictly for the tourists. Indian reservations these days look more like caravan sites. As you fly across the Nevada desert, the Navajo Reservation looks like a huge trailer park, with 4x4 pick-ups parked outside. The truth certainly shatters any romantic notions of the Wild West. But how did the Indians end up in such a predicament - second-class citizens in their own land? The main problem was that they believed the whites' promises. These promises became a liturgy of betrayal. Broken peace and land treaties, attacks on defenceless villages (who were often under white flags), the wanton slaughter of women and children, and the murders of chiefs in white custody was the worst of it. But the presentation of the Indian conflicts down the years, with the whites ridding the land of the 'Red Menace', jars badly with the truth, for the Indian Wars were driven by the whiteman's greed. The promise of a fresh start, gold, farmland or buffalo enticed the settlers into the unknown. To reach these riches, they were willing to incur the wrath of the Indians. When the army intervened, things changed drastically for the Indians. Once the machinery of the dynamic, advanced and fairly ruthless white civilisation was brought to bear against the primitive tribes, there could only be one outcome.

This story reflects and highlights the different facets of the Indian Wars. They range from Indian attacks on unprepared white non-combatants (the Minnesota Massacre) and army attacks on defenceless Indian villages (the Sand Creek Massacre), to more conventional battles, like the Battle of the Rosebud and the Little Big Horn. There are wars started by gold rushes or encroaching railroads, by petty arguments or by murder. There is guerrilla fighting (in the Apache Wars), attempts at pacifism (Chief Joseph's exodus with the Nez Perce) and an examination of the moral choice that faced half-breeds and captives (like the Comanche chief Quanah Parker). According to the Indians, it was the army who usually caused trouble. An old Indian saying goes, 'It was you who sent out the first soldier, and we who sent out the second.' Whatever, the army certainly sent out the most. In the present day Black Hills, not far from the Mount Rushmore presidential carvings, there is another face carved into the hills of South Dakota. In contrast to Washington, Lincoln et al, the face is that of Crazy Horse. The monument was begun in 1949 and in 50 years only his face has been completed. The whole carving will eventually depict the chief riding a horse, so the fact that it's taken the sculptors half a century to finish his face gives you some idea of the scale of the work. The fact that it's still unfinished speaks volumes about attitudes towards the Indians.

Throughout this Pocket Essential Guide I have chosen to refer to the indigenous tribes of North America by the generic name 'Indians', rather than the more widely acceptable 'Native Americans', for a number of reasons. While I fully appreciate that the name 'Indians' is not the preferred term nowadays, it was the name given to the tribes when America was first discovered by Columbus. He thought he had arrived in India and christened the inhabitants 'Indios.' Throughout the American Indian Wars the army's opponents were referred to exclusively as 'Indians' and the mythology of the West is epitomised by the phrase 'Cowboys and Indians', though no offence is intended. I have therefore used the term 'Indians' in an attempt to capture the authentic flavour of the period, as well as to contribute to the fluidity of the text. Moreover, what follows is concerned with the battles, ambushes, atrocities and injustices that constituted the American Indian Wars. There is relatively little about the Native American Indian culture and more about the actual fighting. You won't find out how to make moccasins, string beads or tan buffalo hides, but you will discover how the North American Indians lost in 30 years, what they had owned unchallenged for hundreds.

Wipe-out

'I want you to kill and scalp all, big and little'

The American Civil War of 1861-65 was a pivotal moment in American history for many reasons. It was the first (and last) time the Northern and Southern states of America were involved in a large-scale war on their home turf - the so-called war of 'brother against brother, neighbour against neighbour, father against son.' The war succeeded in abolishing the morally abhorrent exploitation of slaves by the Confederate plantation owners. It was also the only time any Americans suffered the indignity of an occupying force. The defeated South was 'governed' for many years after the war by Northern officials. They were subsequently exploited by crooked traders and exorbitant taxes during the Reconstruction Era. The Civil War also created just the right atmosphere for the Indian Wars to begin in earnest.

During the Civil War, most of the troops were involved in the eastern theatre of war. What happened in the West was of no interest whatsoever to the Easterners, concerned only with the outcome of their own conflict. Across the West, Indians saw the chance to exploit this situation. Settlers were living on the Indians' land, but there were few soldiers to protect them. Now would undoubtedly be the time to seize it back. In the Southern deserts, the Apaches attacked Union and Confederate troops fighting in the area, while further North, the Comanches and Kiowas enjoyed a fruitful period of killing and looting. But the first full-scale Indian War (if a bloody four-week spate of carnage and butchery can be termed as such) was the Minnesota Massacre of 1862.

Little Crow

Like many tribes, the Santee Sioux had found they had had a pretty raw deal when they sold their land to the whites for $1,600,000 in 1851, as part of the Mendota Treaty. They were put on a reservation near the Minnesota River, but while things initially went well, the whites soon lost interest in looking after their charges, and exploitation and avarice began to play a part in the Santee's plight. By 1862, the Indians were in a sorry state. Their food supply was especially problematic, as they had become reliant on white traders, in addition to their own primitive attempts at farming. The crops often failed, while the traders capitalised on the Indians' hunger, selling them any old rubbish. Anger at their treatment was bound to provoke trouble and the Sioux chief Little Crow knew it. Little Crow (also known by the imaginative name 'Hawk That Hunts Walking'), is often described in history books as a 'Christian Indian.' He suffered something of a Damascus Road experience in his youth, changing from an alcoholic philanderer to the epitome of the civilised Indian. He became chief in 1834, lived in a house (rather than a tepee), wore white man's clothes and observed the peace treaty, no matter what the circumstances. A photograph of the time shows how these Indians were suffering an identity crisis. It depicts a placid reservation camp scene. In the background stands a brick house, in the front stands a tepee. The Indian women wear traditional Indian blankets, but the two figures in the centre, a father and son, are dressed in smart frock-coats and clean white shirts (the child is even holding a boater). Their hair is well groomed and neatly parted, and they look decidedly odd compared to the other natives in the photo. But the most chilling aspect of the tranquil scene is that it was taken on the very day that their latent hatred exploded into carnage across the state.

Minnesota Massacre

Accounts differ of how the bloodshed started. What seems certain is that the situation rapidly escalated into full-scale war. The flashpoint was Monday 17 August 1862 in Meeker County. One version maintains that four Indian braves, on their way back from a hunting trip, quarrelled with a settler over some hen's eggs. The white man claimed the Indians were stealing them. Another account prefers that the Indians argued amongst themselves, resulting in a boast along the lines of: 'I'm not scared of whitemen', while another variation states that one of the braves was dared by his friends to murder the settler. Whatever, ten minutes later the pioneer, his wife and daughter, and two neighbours had been shot and scalped. When the tribal leaders learned of the atrocity, they quickly discussed what must be done. Fearing reprisals and figuring that now was as good a time as any to rebel, Little Crow organised what would be the first proper Indian action - a massed attack on the government agency at Redwood Falls.

The Indians took positions overnight and attacked without warning the following morning. Caught completely unawares, the whites were slaughtered where they stood. The traders suffered worst. Any who had treated the Indians unfairly were summarily killed. One trader, who had commented that if the Indians went hungry, they should eat grass, was found later - murdered, scalped and with his mouth stuffed with grass. Townships and smallholdings were attacked at will as the Indians ran riot, completely unopposed. White survivors crossed the river by ferry and headed for Fort Ridgely, running the gauntlet through 15 miles of hostile Sioux country.

The Indians raided outlying settlements stealing provisions, guns and liquor. They captured white women and children, and killed most white men, though they occasionally showed mercy to whites who had treated them decently in the past - sparing a settler who traded livestock with them, a farmer who once gave them food. Estimates of casualties vary significantly, as the conflict was very widespread, but somewhere between 300 to 400 whites were killed in the first days of the 'fighting.' Almost immediately refugees started pouring into Ridgely, a poorly defended stockade that was about to become the focal point for Little Crow's bloody war.

Troops rode from the fort to try and find out what had happened at the agency, but there weren't enough of them to face Little Crow's massed forces. The Commanding officer, Captain March, could only take 48 men from the fort in case of subsequent attack. The token force never reached the agency. They were ambushed at the ferry and in a running retreat lost half their number. March himself drowned in the river. The alarm had also been sent to Fort Snelling, but no reinforcements arrived. Over 20 to 22 August, the Indians attacked the fort, but the delay (they had been looting, burning and getting drunk for the last few days) was crucial. Though their attack was feisty, the defenders were resolute. The Indians repeatedly probed the fort's defences and the situation looked grim. There were almost 300 fugitives packed into the fort, protected by less than 200 volunteers and a smattering of artillery, but it was the artillery that would make the difference. The three day siege was eventually broken when the Indians realised they had no answer to the cannon barrages - in particular canister shot, which had a lethal effect on the tightly packed, charging warriors. Reinforcements from Fort Snelling arrived in the nick of time to bolster the garrison. With the safety of Fort Ridgely secured, the army decided how to discipline the Indians. The hostiles' failure to capture the fort was a major turning point, as the army now had an excellent springboard to launch reprisals in the area. Most of the regular troops were tied up in the east, so the vast majority of forces available were raw recruits and volunteers. Moreover, the towns and outlying settlements were largely undefended and completely open to Little Crow's attacks, which continued unabated.

Following his aborted assault on Fort Ridgely, Little Crow turned his attention to the town of New Ulm, a European settlement with a high percentage of Germanic immigrants. For defence, the whites had about 150 local militia and organised a basic defence strategy for the town. The Sioux came out of the surrounding cornfields on 23 August. The battle raged, seesawing back and forth, but finally the Santee were repulsed, though much of the town was torched. This was less to do with the Indians and more the wishes of the local commander, a judge. He ordered the buildings burned down, rather than let the Sioux take over them, loot them and then use them as cover (to launch subsequent attacks). It was debatable as to who won the engagement. The militia seemed to win, though it was more likely that the Indians got bored with the fight and drifted away. Whatever, New Ulm was saved and the Indians had enough booty for now (including many captives). After New Ulm, there was a lull in the fighting as the Sioux enjoyed their success and assessed what they had achieved - which when it came down to it was very little. They had succeeded in frightening the whites and panicking the entire population for miles around (about 30,000 evacuated the area over the subsequent weeks). But it hardly consolidated their position with the government. They had been starving. Now they were sated. But the whites' retribution would be a heavy price to pay for their fiesta of carnage.

Colonel Sibley was dispatched to quell the rebellion, with a ragtag bunch of 1400 regulars, volunteers and raw recruits. This makeshift army was the best the territory could muster under the circumstances. The Indian raiding continued, but seemed to be losing momentum. Sibley arrived at Fort Ridgely on 28 August and reassured the inhabitants that everything was under control. He then sent out a forage party of 200 men, who rode out to the ferry (witnessing the fate of the last group of soldiers to try to cross the river) and into the bloody aftermath of the agency massacre. There were plenty of corpses and Sibley's men spent their time interring the bodies. Not a particularly pleasant task, as the mutilated cadavers had been lying out in the open, littering the site, for 11 days. The gravediggers came under attack on 1 September, at a place called Birch Coulee. It was only the timely arrival of a larger force under Sibley that saved the day - otherwise the colonel would have spent the next day burying the burial party. It was clear that the Indians were up for a fight again. Sibley spent two weeks deciding how to tackle the Santee. Any wrong move would mean certain death for the hundreds of white prisoners of war, so Sibley had to be cautious. The press misinterpreted this as cowardice and he eventually left Ridgely on 18 September, with 1600 assorted troops and some artillery. The force headed up the Minnesota River Valley towards Little Crow's camp near the Yellow Medicine Indian Agency. Five days later, Sibley neared the camp. Little Crow tried to spring an ambush, but for reasons unknown the troops weren't taken by surprise and repulsed the 700-strong attack. With the Indians at arm's length, Sibley's artillery came into its own. They fired repeatedly into the massed ranks of warriors (who were grouping for an onslaught) and the hostiles eventually gave up and retired from the field, making the Battle of Wood Lake the first white victory of the Indian Wars. Meanwhile, Little Crow, livid in defeat, vowed to slaughter all the captives, but the other chiefs stopped him, saying they could trade them with the government for leniency. But the Indians were deluded if they thought they were going to be let off with a scolding from the authorities.

Sibley wanted the whites back in exchange for amnesty, so the Indians released between 300 and 400 captives on 26 September. There was no enemy as such for the army to track down (they had scattered too far afield), but by the end of October many Santees had given themselves up. The ones who hadn't co-operated were painstakingly rounded up by Sibley's troops. Eventually the army had 2000 captives. 392 were tried and 307 were sentenced to death for their part in the uprising. Bishop Whipple of Minnesota went to President Lincoln and pleaded for reasonable mercy. Eventually Lincoln sentenced only 38 of the worst offenders to death by hanging, the rest of the sentences were commuted. Little Crow's wasn't among the condemned. He had escaped and was in hiding in the hills. The executions took place at Fort Snelling, 26 December 1862. It seemed fitting that these 38 met such a death. The catalogue of horror during the Minnesota Massacre (occasionally dubbed 'The Great Sioux Uprising', though there was nothing particularly 'great' about it) has been well documented. Figures vary, but at least 700 whites were killed. The ferocity and mercilessness of the Indian attacks graphically illustrated how much the Sioux hated the white men. There were the expected atrocities - scalping, rape, burning and mutilation. In addition there was the widespread damage to private property, crops and livestock and the atrocious treatment of hundreds of white captives, some of whom were never seen again. General Pope wrote to the War Department during the unrest: 'You have no idea of the uncontrollable panic everywhere in this country. The most horrible massacres have been committed; children nailed alive to trees and houses; women violated and then disembowelled - everything that horrible ingenuity could devise.' The Indian Wars were violent, uncompromising and savage, but contrary to eastern public opinion, the savages were on both sides. This was proved conclusively by the most notorious massacre in American Western history, the horror that took place at Sand Creek on 29 November 1864.

The Hundred Dazers

The Santee Sioux (now in league with their allies the Teton Sioux) were defeated decisively in a brace of battles - the Battle of Whitestone Hill (September, 1863) and the Battle of Kildeer Mountain (1864). Little Crow himself carried out a few small-scale raids in 1863, but he was ignominiously gunned down by a couple of hunters in the summer while he was picking berries. The lucky pair each received a $25 bounty, plus a $500 reward. More importantly, Little Crow was dead, but elsewhere another atrocity was about to eclipse Little Crow's exploits.

Trouble was brewing in Colorado Territory. Posters had appeared around Denver bearing the slogan 'ATTENTION INDIAN FIGHTERS.' The notice continued that the State governor had been authorised to assemble a company of 'Volunteer Cavalry' to serve for 100 days. Their task was to quell an 'Indian Uprising.' All horses and plunder taken during said actions could be kept by the volunteers. Their formation was a panic measure, as the US government couldn't afford to spare proper troops to fight the Indians. Their commander was Colonel Chivington, a Civil War hero and ex-Methodist preacher, whose name has gone down in the annals of history as the most inhuman, power-hungry and self-motivated individual ever to don the uniform of the US Army (though there were some, especially during the Indian Wars, who came close). In the Indian-hating environment of Denver, with the Minnesota Massacre fresh in everyone's minds, Chivington had little trouble raising his Volunteer Cavalry of fearless Indian Fighters.

The so-called 'Indian Uprising' was little more than a half-baked reaction by local Cheyenne and Arapahos to an invasion by gold-hungry prospectors. In 1858, gold had been discovered at Pike's Peak, which led to a rush of gold miners (or rather budding gold miners), eager to make their fortunes. The Indians were irritated by this influx and by 1864 they were determined to push the invaders out. The Cheyenne were led by a chief named Black Kettle (Indian name Moketavata), who was a strong believer in a peaceful resolution of the problem, but other tribal factions wanted war. Two versions exist of how the conflict started. One claims that the Indians tired of their unwanted white visitors and declared war. The other says that Chivington, then commander of the 1st Colorado Regiment, had discovered that the Cheyenne had rustled 175 cattle from a rancher nearby and wanted to retaliate. It was the perfect excuse to attack the Indians, but it was revealed long after the event that no such rustling had taken place. In the spring the fighting escalated and the Indians began raiding through Colorado, raising alarm among the inhabitants. With lines of communication cut, Denver was virtually besieged. The Indians brutally murdered a settler, his wife, four-year-old daughter and baby. The corpses were exhibited in Denver and the locals were outraged, calling for protection against the hostiles. In answer to their pleas, Territorial Governor Evans allowed the formation of a militia, the 3rd Colorado Volunteers. The reason the governor mustered them so readily was twofold. Firstly, the area was very low on troops (with the Civil War sapping valuable military resources) and a volunteer cavalry would get rid of the Indians and allow the locals a chance to get back at the hostiles. But more importantly, Evans harboured political ambitions and putting down a rebellion would look good on his CV. Colonel Chivington also had his greedy eyes on a political career and was in cahoots with Evans. Chivington would lead the 3rd to glorious victory and Evans would become State Governor, a highly prestigious position. There was a catch - Evans only had permission to enlist the volunteers for 100 days. After that they would be disbanded. And to make matters worse the Indians had stopped their attacks. It looked like peace was on the horizon.

Black Kettle had struck a deal with the other chiefs to meet the commander of Fort Lyon, an outpost in the locality. There, they had been assured protection by the army, if they discontinued their raids. It was November 1864, with winter fast approaching, and the Indians thought it would be sensible to cease raiding (which was being done by small groups of hotheads). Earlier in the year, Chivington had led the 1st Colorado Regulars (no relation to their ragtag cousins, the Volunteer 3rd) against the Indians, and had destroyed several Cheyenne camps. Often these camps had no connection whatsoever with the hostilities, but Chivington was indiscriminate. The Indians didn't want this to continue and so complied with the whites' offer. Under the army's protection they would camp at Sand Creek, about forty miles from Fort Lyon and peacefully spend the winter there. But Evans and Chivington had other plans. The Volunteer Cavalry's 100 days had nearly expired. They had to be used fast, or Evans would be a laughing stock. The locals were starting to call the 'Hundred Dazers' the 'Bloodless Third' for their lack of action. Chivington, with his 700 troops and some artillery, first went to Fort Lyon and surrounded the stockade, so that no one could leave and warn the Indians. Then he purloined a guide to lead them to Sand Creek. At 8pm on 28 November, the column moved out towards the camp. It soon became obvious that their 69-year-old guide's eyesight wasn't very good and Chivington enlisted a local rancher to lead them, who was half Cheyenne himself. At dawn they were upon Black Kettle's camp. Chivington gave the order to attack the village and the tragedy commenced.

Sand Creek Massacre

What the troops thought they were attacking was a 'hostile' Indian village. What they were actually attacking was a peaceful camp, with few warriors present. Most of the men were off hunting buffalo before the harsh winter set in. In fact, the 500 Cheyenne were mostly women, children and elders. Chivington had instructed his rabble to kill everyone they found, regardless of age or sex, reasoning, "Nits make lice." The Cheyenne were awoken by the approaching troops. The village was laced with cannon shots and bullets, while the Indians scrambled for cover. There were about 200 warriors in the camp, but they were poorly armed - they had handed much of their arsenal over to the army during the peace talks. Nevertheless they managed to mount a rough defence so the women and children could escape. Black Kettle raised the American flag on a pole near his tepee. It had been a present from President Lincoln on a peace mission years before. Beneath it he hoisted a white flag. These two symbols of pacifism did nothing for his chances. The soldiers slaughtered as many Indians as they could find. Babies were crushed, women knifed, the elderly ridden down and shot. The Indians pleaded for mercy and the soldiers showed none. In the frenzy, the whites mutilated the Indians in the same grotesque manner the Cheyenne had mutilated their kinfolk. Apart from scalping, bodies were torn apart with knives in indescribable ways. The savagery was such that some of Chivington's officers were so appalled they refused to take part in the action and were consequently accused of cowardice (!). One officer, Captain Soule, recalled seeing children on their knees begging for their lives, only to be slaughtered where they knelt, among many other atrocities. Miraculously, the few armed Indians managed to hold the troops at bay so that many of their families could escape. With the camp overrun, the troops completed their dirty work and found among the debris vindication for their actions. Bags and bales stuffed with white scalps - blond, brunette and red, some with pretty ringlets, others with long flowing locks. It seemed Chivington was right to assault the village. The reports of Indian casualties vary. Around 100 women and children were killed, in addition to 30 warriors. Black Kettle made an escape with his wife, even though she was shot nine times. Chivington's casualties were negligible.

After the attack, Chivington and his men rode back to Denver to report their heroics. The locals were ecstatic that their foray had been a resounding success. The troops were decorated with mementoes of the fight. Dripping scalps dangled from poles, while body parts adorned hats, saddles and jackets like gory trophies. It must have been a ghastly sight to witness the return of the Third. Scalps were put on show around the town and the press went wild. The Rocky Mountain News reported: 'Great Battle With Indians - The Savages Dispersed'. It continued that 'Colorado soldiers have covered themselves with glory' (not to mention entrails), while other local publications were similarly celebratory. Others, especially in the East, were less impressed. Slowly, through officers' gossip and unconfirmed reports from 'Indian lovers' in the area, it was obvious that this glorious action was nothing of the sort. The Indians were peaceful and thought they were under the army's protection. They hadn't even posted any guards on the camp, and most importantly they had raised a white flag and tried to surrender. The government investigated the action, but suddenly there was no one to blame. Chivington resigned soon afterwards (though his career, political or otherwise, was ruined) and the Hundred Dazers' hundred days were up. The inquiry could not try anyone and some of the other crucial witnesses either refused to testify or couldn't. Key source Captain Soule, who had openly opposed the attack, was murdered before he could appear. Some history books have the nerve to note Sand Creek in the index under 'Battles', which is a huge compliment to the action. It was a premeditated slaughter of defenceless people, who were served up as a sacrifice to further the careers of a few fanatically ambitious men. When the truth came out, the massacre could finally be seen for what it was. Also Easterners, so apathetic to Indian matters before, were now fully aware of the ferocity of Indian warfare. Chivington had said to his men before the massacre, "I want you to kill and scalp all, big and little." They sound like the words of a savage. And they were - except this one was white.

Black Hills Run Red

'Now I, who used to control 5000 warriors, must tell
Washington when I am hungry'

Following the white atrocities at the Sand Creek Massacre, the Indians wanted bloody revenge for the Cheyenne women and children murdered under a flag of truce. Obligingly, in the years following the Civil War, there were a lot more whites to attack. With the end of the War in the east, more troops were available to man the frontier forts, and settlers felt a little safer when the bluecoat reinforcements arrived in the area. The abundance of invaders only fuelled the antagonistic atmosphere and drove the Indians to assemble their biggest fighting force yet. As the area filled with farmers and the buffalo herds scattered, the Indian raids got worse and it was decided by the government that desperate action must be taken. But what the councillors and politicians didn't realise was that these raids were being carried out by some of the greatest warriors ever to fight the army.

Red Cloud's War

Red Cloud, of the Teton branch of the Sioux, was their leader and tribal figurehead. He was also known by his Indian name Makhpiyaluta. Born about 1822, he had risen to prominence in 1863 and though there were many different Indian factions about to wage war on the whites, he united them in their hatred. In council with the whites, he spoke honestly for them and the Sioux and Cheyenne followed him. He was also the only chief ever to win an Indian war against the bluecoats. One of the hottest spots on the frontier in the post-Civil War West was the Bozeman Trail (also called the Powder River Trail). This trail wound from Fort Laramie, Wyoming, all the way to the Montana gold mines (near Virginia City). It was essential that it be kept open for the miners and settlers to travel it safely. Red Cloud wanted it closed. The trail cut straight through Sioux country, disrupting the pattern of their lives. More importantly, the constant wagon trains disturbed the buffalo herds, a most precious commodity to the Indians. So they began harassing wagon trains, raiding camps, killing and scalping - in the Cheyenne's case in revenge for the barbarity of Colonel Chivington and company. In the Sioux's case, for the flagrant disregard for the latest in a long line of treaties.

In 1866 things had got so bad that the government called for a Peace Council meeting in June, again to be held at Fort Laramie. All the tribal leaders attended and were duly bribed with gunpowder, lead and food - the first two were perhaps not the best things to give warlike Indians. Things weren't going too badly around the peace table, until it emerged that whatever the outcome, the government planned to occupy the Bozeman Trail area anyway. This became glaringly apparent when Colonel Carrington and a column of 700 men arrived. They were on their way to begin building stockades along the trail, to house the troops needed to protect the settlers. The army had a full array of construction equipment in tow, including brick-making machines and a steam-powered sawmill. It was obvious that Carrington wasn't going to be building a moonlight camp, but something altogether more solid. Red Cloud went berserk when he saw this and curtailed the talks immediately. But Sioux chief Spotted Tail and several others stayed and agreed a peace treaty - as far as they were concerned, Carrington could get on with his job. But if the whites thought they could treat the Sioux and Cheyenne this way, they hadn't counted on Red Cloud. In his mind, it could only be resolved one way. Outright war.

Blood On The Bozeman

Taking no notice of Red Cloud's threats, the army began to construct a trio of forts along the Bozeman. Heading north, the first was the revamped Fort Connor (renamed Fort Reno) and beyond that, the last to be built was Fort C F Smith. But it was the fort that was sited between the two, at the foot of the Bighorn Mountains, that bore the brunt of the Indians' anger. Work began on Fort Phil Kearny (as it was named) in July 1866. Carrington was the perfect choice for this risky construction exercise. He was a soldier by trade, but also an engineer. Once the site was chosen, work began, but it was apparent that Red Cloud and his renegade allies weren't about to let the soldiers and carpenters work unmolested. The work parties were constantly harassed and many labourers and guards were picked-off at will. The problem was that though the fort was to be built in an excellent position for defence (and useful commodities like grass and water), the timber needed to build the stockade was a long way away - seven hazardous miles. Every time a woodcutting party left the protection of the troops, the Indians would strike. Only a token escort ever accompanied the lumber teams, lest the defence itself be overrun. Diarists of the time, including Carrington's wife, painted a miserable picture of life in the nascent Phil Kearny. Wagon trains were chased and attacked, and sentries wounded or even worse, captured.

Mrs Carrington wrote on 13 September 1866 that during the night the alarm was raised that the hay contractors had been attacked. One man had been killed, cattle had been run-off and hay had been torched atop five mowing machines. Three days later an outrider was cut-off and dragged away by Indians, never to be seen again. On the 27 September a soldier was scalped, then crawled half a mile to the stockade, and two lumber workers were attacked and scalped in front of their fellow workers. Both sides received reinforcements, but even with a force of 300, Carrington was still hopelessly outnumbered. Red Cloud and Dull Knife's forces were swelled by contingents of Arapaho, Sioux and Cheyenne, including the soon-to-be famous names, Roman Nose and the Oglala warrior Crazy Horse. Though several sources claim Sitting Bull was also present, he was actually fighting elsewhere. Fort Phil Kearny was finished by the end of October, but the men who had toiled so hard to complete the structure soon realised they had built little more than their own prison. They were effectively under permanent siege. Under strength, Carrington was cautious and let the Indians raid and loot any outlying commands with scant resistance. A sustained thrust would leave the fort open to a potentially fatal attack. Several of Carrington's officers were disillusioned with his overly prudent approach and wanted to show the Redskins what they were made of. If they had only known how soon they would get the opportunity.

Fetterman's Folly

Among the cocky officers was Captain Fetterman, who arrived at the fort in November. Convinced the Indians were little more than rabble, he claimed that with 80 good men he could defeat the whole Sioux nation. His zeal for combat was echoed by Captain Brown, who said that given the chance he would claim Red Cloud's scalp. This big talk worried Carrington, who was having enough trouble running a lumber operation and trying to keep the Bozeman open - he was failing miserably on both counts. On 6 December Fetterman got his chance to face the Indians. A signaller told the fort that a lumber train (sent to fell pine) was under attack. Fetterman rode out to the rescue, with 30 men, while Carrington skirted around with another 14 men to try and outflank the hostiles. Fetterman, pursuing a small band of Indians, rode straight past the lumber team and gave chase. But it was a trap. The entire party was completely surrounded and outnumbered, and it was only the timely arrival of Carrington's small contingent that scattered the Indians and saved the day. Fetterman was admonished, but it seemed to have little effect. The Indian forays continued almost daily, while Red Cloud planned his most audacious attack yet. On 19 December they attacked and goaded a force under Captain Powell, but Powell was no idiot and refused to be drawn. On Friday 21 December, at about 11 o'clock on a freezing cold day, a signaller again broke the grim news that the loggers were under fire. Fetterman got command of the relief column. He led the 48 infantrymen, Lieutenant Grummond led 29 cavalry. Two civilians armed with 16-shot Henry rifles saddled-up as the troops left and went along. Unbelievably Fetterman had exactly 80 men. But could he deliver on his boast?

The simple and unsurprising answer is no. With explicit orders from Carrington not to follow the Indians beyond a hill called Lodge Trail Ridge, Fetterman set off. He didn't head straight for the wood train, but instead followed the Indians who had stopped their attack and turned their attention to luring the troops further from the fort. It never occurred to the vain Fetterman that these Indians weren't running very fast. They were led by a cunning young warrior named Crazy Horse and they didn't bother to rush. Fetterman, blinded by his ego, fell for the ruse. He followed them up the slope of Lodge Trail Ridge, over the brow and out of sight of the fort. Filled with foreboding, Carrington watched from the stockade and could see Indians milling about in the grass around the ridge. Once the troops were on the other side of the ridge, all was confusion. The decoys led Fetterman into one almighty trap, with 2000 warriors waiting in the valley and beyond. They came from all sides and slaughtered the command to a man. All the fort knew of the engagement was the volleys of shots that started around noon. Carrington assembled a 115-man relief column, with wagons, under Captain Ten Eyck and sent them to help Fetterman. With such a large force away, the fort was undefended and every spare hand was needed, including prisoners released from the guardhouse. Ten Eyck gave Fetterman's route a wide berth and rode to a nearby hilltop to see what had happened. All he could see in the valley below was hundreds and hundreds of war-painted, shrieking savages. And they were in celebratory mood.

Ten Eyck returned at nightfall with dreadful news and an even worse cargo. He informed Carrington that Fetterman's entire force has been massacred and that he had managed to collect the remains of 49 frozen, naked, mutilated corpses as macabre proof. The night spent in the fort was the stuff of nightmares. Carrington was convinced the Indians would attack and wipe out the fort. He even issued orders that if it looked as though the outpost would be overwhelmed, the women and children should be taken to the ammunition store and blown-up, to save an ordeal at the hands of the Sioux and Cheyenne. But extremely bad weather saved the day. The temperature dropped to minus 30° and the Indians went to ground. The following day Carrington dispatched a scout named 'Portugee' Phillips (an exotic character, who was of Portuguese ancestry) to Fort Laramie for help. Meanwhile the colonel went out with a party of troops to retrieve the rest of the bodies. The battlefield was a gruesome sight. All the whites had been stripped, cut-up, scalped, disembowelled, brained or blinded…the barbaric liturgy went on. Both Grummond and Fetterman had powder-burns to the temple, signifying they had committed suicide. The Indians loathed Captain Brown so much that they had even scalped his horse. Only a young bugler had been spared the mutilation - he had fought bravely, fending off the Indians with his bugle, which was found battered out of all recognition nearby. Instead of being slashed to ribbons, he had a buffalo robe placed over his body, as a mark of respect. Messenger Phillips arrived at Fort Reno against all the odds and then rode on to Laramie, interrupting the Christmas Eve ball with the dreadful news of the Fetterman Massacre. Reinforcements were dispatched, but the winter was hard on both sides and the fighting resumed the following year. The Bozeman was still effectively closed, as Indians made sure no one got through. Moreover, though Phil Kearny had to endure the brunt of the fighting, both Forts Reno and C F Smith had a rough time too - the men at Smith were besieged with no contact with the outside world from November 1866 to March 1867. The Fetterman Massacre was a huge setback for the army and Carrington was relieved of his command in January 1867. As commanding officer, he took the blame for the defeat, even though Fetterman disobeyed orders and wantonly led his soldiers to oblivion. In Indian circles the massacre was called 'The Battle of the Hundred Slain', which wasn't an indication that the Indians couldn't count, but was named after a Sioux 'winkte' prophesy. A 'winkte' was a warrior who dressed and spoke like a woman, and was thought to have mysterious powers. The one who rode with the Sioux enacted the battle for the huge assembled ambush party before the clash actually took place. He foretold that they would slaughter 100 soldiers, hence the name.

Burned Out

Carrington's replacement was Colonel Wessells, who found the going no easier than his predecessor. The enemies sniped at each other throughout the winter and the war resumed in July 1867, with Crazy Horse raiding at Fort Reno. The Indian tribes then divided into two groups. The Cheyennes turned their attention to Fort C F Smith, while the Sioux concentrated on Phil Kearny. The Cheyenne attacked a gang of hay-makers on 1 August. But the troops, though outnumbered over fifteen to one, were now armed with new breach-loading Springfield rifles that could fire far more rapidly than the old single-shot models. Shocked, the Indians withdrew and the encounter became known as the Hayfield Fight, though it is the next day's events that are more often recounted in history books. A timber fell-ing party from Phil Kearney was attacked by a huge force of Indians on 2 August. The woodcutters escaped to the fort, but their escort, 30 men under Captain Powell, took cover in a makeshift stockade, a ring of wagon beds (called wagon boxes) removed from their wheels. Again the soldiers were armed with some excellent hardware - a selection of Colt revolvers and Springfields, with a smattering of Spencer repeaters. Against them rode 500 warriors under Crazy Horse. Wave after wave of braves stormed the little fortress, but the well-armed defenders repulsed them every time with an unrelenting fusillade. The Indians called the whites' weapons 'medicine guns', because they seemed to possess magic powers. A sustained Indian attack on foot and an attempt to burn them out also failed, and the troops were eventually saved by the arrival of a relief column packing a howitzer. The army lost 7 dead, 2 wounded (some sources claim only 6 dead) at the Wagon Box Fight, while Indian casualties were very heavy. Estimates ranged from 60 to 180 dead, and many more wounded, which was catastrophic for Red Cloud. Many of the Indians now lost interest in the war, but the stranglehold on the forts was sustained. For another winter whites were unable to use the Bozeman.

So in April 1868, the government opened talks with Red Cloud as to how they could come to a mutually satisfying agreement. The chief wanted nothing less than the complete banishment of whites from the area. All settlers, miners, traders and soldiers were to keep off the Bozeman Trail and the trio of forts must be abandoned. Amazingly, the whites agreed, provided work could continue on the Northern Pacific Railroad. With his demands met, Red Cloud, Crazy Horse et al watched while the forts were abandoned. As the troops pulled out, the Indians gleefully burned the hated stockades to the ground. The army had constructed them in an effort to 'police' the Indians in their own territory and the plan had completely floundered. At last the Indians' land was their own, or so they thought. In November, Red Cloud rode into Fort Laramie and signed a peace treaty, while other breakaway factions, including Crazy Horse's band, declined to attend. Red Cloud was convinced that he had defeated the entire US Army, but two years later, to show him exactly what he was up against, the government invited him to Washington DC. There he saw the true might of the invader. He also addressed a pro-Indian rally in the New York Cooper Institute and received a rousing reception. But thereafter, he was somewhat cowed at the enormous resources available to the whites. One thing's for sure - Red Cloud the war chief was no more. Elsewhere, his one-time ally, Crazy Horse, took up the fight. His war with the whites would continue and it was ironic that Crazy Horse was finally persuaded to give himself up at the Red Cloud Agency, by his old friend, the great chief himself. Red

Cloud died in 1909. He was one of the classic chiefs, who fully exploited the simple tactic of the ambush and his short, bloody, and enormously effective, war on the Bozeman Trail assured him a place in history.

White Red Man

'If my mother could learn the ways of the Indian, I can learn the
ways of the whiteman'

Chief Quanah of the Comanches was something of an exception to the
other Indian leaders. Not only was he an extremely learned man (who after
his defeat became a political figure and a judge), he was also fighting
against his own ancestors, the whites. For Quanah was a half-breed, born of
a white mother and a Comanche father, who adopted his mother's surname
'Parker' in later civilised life. Blood is thicker than water, but Quanah's
was mixed - white and red. Having been raised as the son of a Comanche
chief, he naturally led his red brothers in a vicious war to drive the destruc-
tive buffalo hunters, meddlesome settlers and intrusive soldiers from their
land. These quarrels culminated in the Red River War of 1874-1875, often
referred to as the War of the Staked Plains. Moreover, the story of the
Comanche clashes with the army are inexorably linked to the Comanches'
allies, the Kiowas, and it is with the Comanches' northern neighbours that
Quanah's story begins.

White Bear and Sitting Bear

The Kiowas had been fighting the whites in the area since the 1820's,
and treaties had come and gone. The reasons for their failure were familiar
to every Indian on the plains. The biggest increase in white traffic came
with the California Gold Rush of 1848, which opened the floodgates for the
white invasion. This resulted in a steady stream of wagons throughout the
1850's. Kiowas and Comanches, allies since the late 1700's, wouldn't
stand for such trespassing and set about raiding and looting the travellers.
In Texas the Indian attacks were so feared that the Texas Rangers had been
formed and their innovative Indian fighting tactics resulted in daring raids
into Comanche territory, often to rescue white captives, destroy villages or
confiscate gunrunners' merchandise. The Kiowas were led by Little Mountain. The Civil War years (1861-1865), saw the ferocity of their raids
increase. Towards the end of the Civil War, things were beginning to get
out of hand along the Santa Fe Trail. Kiowas swooped at will and the
whites decided it was time for retaliation. Colonel Kit Carson led a force of
about 400 men and two howitzers into the Texas Panhandle area, with a
view to launching a surprise attack. This action turned out to be far more
effective than the government could have hoped. On 25 November 1864,
Carson struck at Little Mountain's camp at Adobe Walls and in a day-long

battle he razed the camp to the ground, captured livestock and routed the enemy. He had achieved this even though he was vastly outnumbered (there were about 1000 warriors involved in the encounter). It was the end for Little Mountain, who died the following year and left the Kiowas torn between two very different leaders. Little Mountain had made peace with the whites, but one of their new leaders, White Bear (sometimes called Santana) was a warrior and disagreed with the other candidate for tribal leader, Kicking Bird (who was an advocate for peace). This power play would manifest itself most obviously at the Medicine Lodge Creek peace summit of 1867. While Red Cloud and the Northern Plains Indians were expected at the powwow at Fort Laramie, the Southern tribes (Kiowa, Arapahos, Cheyenne and Comanche) met government representatives at Medicine Lodge Creek. White Bear was particularly vocal about the wanton slaughter of the buffalo and in the short term the cull appeared to subside.

The Indians signed the treaty, for what it was worth, but their treatment by the whites, particularly an inconsistent food supply, led to further unrest. By 1870, Kicking Bird could no longer hold his peace stance. Gradually White Bear and the older Sitting Bear (also known as Santank) goaded him into war. Accused of cowardice, Kicking Bear led a war party from their reservation into Texas and caused havoc, raiding stage stations, clashing with the cavalry and stealing horses. Kicking Bear had saved face, but it wasn't enough for White Bear. In May 1871, White Bear, Sitting Bear and the seer Sky Walker (sometimes referred to as Mamanti, or 'The Owl') again raided into Texas, leading about 100 braves. They were preparing to attack a small party of soldiers (actually General Sherman on an inspection tour of the area) when Sky Walker predicted that richer pickings would soon arrive. The ambush was postponed and sure enough a wagon train transporting grain hove into view. The attack was successful, with the Kiowas slaughtering at will and making a clean getaway with their booty. But weeks later three of the raiders - White Bear, Sitting Bear and Big Tree - inadvertently let slip that they had carried out the bloody attack. Troops were dispatched to arrest the perpetrators. The murderous trio were tricked into a rendezvous, then captured and taken to Fort Sill. From there they were handcuffed in wagons and transported to Jacksboro in Texas. On the way, the elderly warrior Sitting Bear made a suicidal break for it and was shot dead, while the other two were subsequently sentenced to hang. Amazingly, the governor later pardoned the pair and they were paroled in August 1873. With peace brought to the Kiowa bands, the younger members drifted away from their reservation and threw in with the Kwahadi band of Comanche led by a notorious half-breed raider named Quanah.

Quanah - A Breed Apart

Like the Kiowas, the Comanches had raided throughout Texas (similarly proving particularly problematic during the Civil War years), though their war with the whitemen had been dragging on for much longer than that. In 1836 the Indians had attacked Parker's Fort in Texas and had ridden off with five captives - two women, Mrs Kellog and Mrs Plummer, plus Mrs Plummer's baby son and two young kids, John Parker and his 9 year-old sister Cynthia Ann. The women were later ransomed, but the children were not. Cynthia Ann adapted to life with the Comanches and eventually became the wife of the chief, Peta Nocona. She bore him three children - two sons, Quanah and Pecos, and a daughter, Prairie Flower. Quanah grew-up to become a strong warrior, sure to be a future chief. In 1860, a troop of Texas Rangers attacked their largely undefended camp (many of the warriors were away hunting) and managed to free Cynthia Ann and her daughter, though she wasn't very willing to be liberated. Now 33, she had grown used to the Indian ways and would never learn how to live in a 'civilised' society. Despite her protests, she was taken back to live with her natural family in East Texas. Unhappy, she attempted to escape on numerous occasions. Tragedy struck in 1864, when Prairie Flower died of a fever and, unable to contemplate living without her daughter, Cynthia Ann starved herself to death. Soon after his mother was taken away by the whites, Quanah lost both his father and his brother, so he abandoned his father's people and joined the Kwahadi faction, on the Llano Estacado or 'Staked Plains.'

During the Civil War the Comanches massacred many settlers and the government brokered peace. Like Little Mountain's Kiowas, the Comanche attended the Medicine Lodge Creek council in 1867, though Quanah himself didn't bother to go. He was enjoying the war and would do anything in his power to prolong it. He had also recently learned of the death of his mother and though she was a white, he blamed her 'rescuers' for her ultimate fate. His own personal war would continue, even though many Comanches and Kiowas signed the treaty. Quanah now had a ready supply of guns and ammunition, which were being sold across the frontier by Mexican and gringo lowlife traders, the so-called 'Comancheros'. The government quickly realised the peace treaty wasn't worth the paper it was written on and Colonel Mackenzie, commander of Fort Richardson, was instructed to put a stop to the wanton Indian raids in Texas. He began by sending out patrols, to reconnoitre and keep the Comanches on their toes (a measure that was later used to subdue the Apache Indians, who inhabited a similarly barren landscape). In October 1871 Quanah's Kwahadis attacked an army outpost and ran off some horses. Mackenzie rode a column of 600 men into the Staked Plains to track them down. The whole exercise was a complete failure in its actual objectives (i.e. stopping the raids), but Mackenzie learned much from his terrible experiences in the inhospitable country and the next time he was called upon to get Quanah, he was better prepared.

Staked-Out On The Plains

In early 1872, Mackenzie's campaign resumed with a vengeance, tackling the Comanches and cutting off their gun supplies from the Comancheros. Mackenzie was backed up by another flying column under Lieutenant Colonel Shafter and this time the troops were more successful. On 29 September Mackenzie struck in his most decisive attack yet. Riding from Fort Richardson, he surprised a Kotsoteka Comanche village of 260 tepees on McClellan Creek, killing about 40 warriors, and capturing 120 women and children, and a large horse herd. Unfortunately, before Mackenzie could get the horses to the fort, the Comanches ambushed his column and stole them back. However, Mackenzie's valuable hostages were put to tactical use and their kinfolk quit raiding, lest the captives were harmed. Some even gave themselves up, including Chief Mow-way's band, whose village had been attacked. But the emotional leverage of the hostages was lost when the authorities misinterpreted this lull in hostilities as a sign of peace. No sooner were the hostages released than the Comanche forays restarted, with even more venom. Kiowa chief Lone Wolf lost his son in the subsequent skirmishes and was eager for white blood, while Quanah's hatred seemed worse than ever. White captives were horribly tortured, burned or left staked-out in the sun for the vultures. These acts of brutality seem to have left Quanah unaffected, even though he was of partially white ancestry. As far as he was concerned, he knew exactly which side he was fighting for, with no questions of morality. Early in 1874, the Comanches and Kiowas cemented their brotherhood with a Sun Dance ceremony. The Kwahadi Comanche chief Bull Bear and his lieutenant Quanah were fully aware that the Kiowas were valuable allies. In particular, the Kiowa chief White Bear, recently released from prison, was keen to prove to his men that he wasn't cowed by white power. Partisan warriors from other bands, including Cheyenne and Arapaho, also sided with the alliance.

Quanah had an ace up his sleeve - a medicine man called Isatai (which translates as the unflattering 'Coyote Droppings'). In an outrageous claim, Isatai told the assembled Indians that he had 'learned from the Great Gods' how to make bullet-proof warpaint. Some sources also add that he could stop bullets mid-flight with his powerful 'good medicine.' Quanah smelled a rat (or could it be coyote droppings?) in the medicine man's boast, but went along with the prophet, knowing such fervour would provoke a feeling of optimism and bravery. The warriors were jubilant and the time had come for action on the Staked Plains. Over the last few months buffalo hunters had appeared in the area. They had begun to slaughter and skin hundreds of animals, then ship the pelts back East where there was a high demand for leather goods and clothes. The base of this barbaric operation was the settlement of Adobe Walls (where Kit Carson had attacked the Kiowas in 1864), but this time it would be the Indians who were doing the attacking. It was decided that the hunters at Adobe Walls would take the brunt of the now-invincible, bullet-proof Comanche and Kiowa army. 700 fierce warriors against a besieged handful of 28 grizzled buffalo hunters. There could only be one outcome.

Quanah allowed Isatai to lead the allied Indian forces in a dawn raid on the hunters' camp. It was 26 June 1874, nearly two years to the day before the Battle of the Little Bighorn. There were three deciding factors in the outcome of the Battle of Adobe Walls (Act II). The first was that the buffalo hunters knew their trade - if there was one thing they were good at, it was shooting at a fast-moving target. The second was that the hunters were toting long barrelled, heavy calibre Sharps rifles with telescopic sights - ideal for blasting Indians out of the saddle at long or short-range. And the third crucial factor was that Isatai, aka Coyote Droppings, lived up to his name. The paint wasn't invulnerable, and Isatai would have needed sheets of plate steel to stop the Sharps ammunition in mid-air. Alerted by a mysterious noise (a loud crack) the sleeping hunters awoke to see Isatai's forces creeping stealthily towards the blockhouses. But Adobe Walls was well-named and the structure, a cluster of buildings and a few low, fortress-like adobe walls, made the place highly defensible. Attack after attack was repulsed during the three-day siege by the deadly marksmen with their heavy bore, precision guns. Weight of numbers, bravery and self-belief weren't enough and the Indians eventually conceded that the hunters were just too good for them. After the battle, only 13 Indian bodies were found scattered around the site, though their casualties would have been many more. Three hunters had been killed and the white survivors cut the heads off the Indian corpses and impaled their trophies on poles around the base, as a grim reminder for the Indians should they try to overwhelm Adobe Walls again. The heavy defeat was largely blamed on Isatai's inaccurate powers of prophecy, rather than Quanah's tactics. Quanah had been wounded in the encounter by a magic, invisible bullet (actually a ricochet) while another warrior had been shot out of the saddle by one of the hunters (named Billy Dixon) who was positioned a mile away - an astonishing distance and a truly amazing piece of marksmanship. The Indian retribution was widespread and bloody, as they reverted to their more familiar targets - settlers, wagon trains, army patrols - targets that were much simpler to defeat than the buffalo hunters at Adobe Walls.

Red River War

Throughout the spring and early summer of 1874, the Indian allies avenged their dead. Lone Wolf took vengeance for the death of his son by ambushing a group of Texas Rangers. In July General Sherman declared war on the hostile bands. He sent a message to General Sheridan to resume the fight in earnest and the Red River War was officially begun. Though five columns were mobilised (from Forts Sill, Bascom, Concho, Richardson and Dodge), Mackenzie was again in the thick of the action. He was assigned to scour the Staked Plains and kill or capture Quanah and his followers. Other columns were commanded by Colonel Miles (a comparative newcomer to the plains, but later one of the best Indian fighters of all), Colonel 'Black Jack' Davidson, Major Price and Lieutenant Buell. On 26 September Mackenzie suffered an ineffective night attack, but on the morning of 28 September, he learned that a large force of Comanches, Kiowas and Cheyenne were hiding in a deep chasm, called the Palo Duro Canyon (also known by the evocative name 'Place of the Chinaberry Trees'). The Indians thought they were safe from attack, but out of the blue Mackenzie struck. He rode his 600 men through the camp, the Indians scattered and Mackenzie was able to capture over 1500 horses. Having learned his lessons in the past, Mackenzie wasn't going to risk losing his booty this time. In an unprecedented, barbaric move he ordered the mounts herded to the Tule Canyon. There he slaughtered 1000 of them, making use of the finest steeds and relieving the Indians of their transportation. There was no need for Mackenzie and the other columns to press their advantage. The colonel knew that the Indians couldn't survive without horses - that much he had learned from his previous campaigns. He also burned their homes and laid waste their food supplies. It was only a matter of time before they started rolling into the reservations. By October 1874 the first Comanches and Kiowas began to arrive before the winter set in, but Quanah wasn't one of the refugees. He and his band had not been caught in the Palo Duro ambush and hadn't lost any of their supplies and livestock. Elsewhere, Kicking Bird the Kiowa had stayed peaceful during the hostilities, while White Bear and Big Tree had been dogged by the army since the Red River offensive began. They, like Quanah, were still holding out. The two renegade Kiowas were eventually convinced to give themselves up by Kicking Bird and capitulated on 3 October. White Bear and Big Tree were still technically only on parole, so when they did eventually surrender, their sentences were harsh (including a life sentence for White Bear). With his comrades back on the reservation, Lone Wolf and his followers arrived in February 1875, after enduring a hard winter. In June, Mackenzie finally made contact with Quanah and offered to let him surrender. Quanah, now aged 30 and having seen the buffalo herds depleted, the devastating effects of the whites' guns on his warriors and his allies taken into captivity, agreed to turn himself in.

Quanah arrived at the reservation and Colonel Mackenzie rode out to meet him from Fort Sill. With Quanah's declaration, the Red River War ended on 2 June 1875. But Quanah's history-making wasn't finished yet and for the next three decades he did what he could for the Indians' lot. As Quanah himself said, "If my mother could learn the ways of the Indian, I can learn the ways of the whiteman." In the entrepreneurial spirit, he charged cattle barons a dollar a head to move their herds across reservation land. Then he went further and rented large areas of the Comanches' land to the ranchers for grazing. The revenue was an excellent asset for the often starving Indians. But as larger tracts of land were opened up for colonisation, the government caught on to Quanah's scheme and in 1892 their land area was severely reduced. Nevertheless, Quanah continued his good (and more importantly peaceful) work. Among Quanah's other achievements in his reservation years was that he was elected deputy sheriff of the town of Lawton (in Oklahoma Territory), had a town named after him, became a school district president and later even a judge, on a special Court of Indian Offences. All this he accomplished under the name Quanah Parker, having adopted his mother's surname in 1878. Soon after his capture he became curious as to his cultural roots and in a variation on 'meet the ancestors' he travelled to East Texas. There among the whitemen, he met his mother's Uncle Silas and stayed at the family home for a while, before returning to his true home with his own people. There, after such an extraordinary, rewarding and fruitful life, he died peacefully of pneumonia in 1911.

Many of the other participants of the Red River War weren't so lucky. Lone Wolf, the Kiowa chief, died of malaria in 1878. Chief Kicking Bird had recommended that the troublemakers Lone Wolf and the seer Sky Walker be taken to prison in Fort Marion, Florida. Kicking Bird died bent double in agony two days later, supposedly from a hex placed on him by Sky Walker (though an autopsy revealed that the coffee Kicking Bird had been drinking was laced with poison). The prophet himself died in prison shortly afterwards, having been overcome with remorse for the power of his own 'magic.' Meanwhile in late 1878, White Bear dealt with his lonely imprisonment (cooped-up in Huntsville prison), by chanting a death chant and throwing himself out of a second floor window. But the most amazing story is that of the notorious Kiowa renegade, Big Tree. Taking the term 'rehabilitation' to the extreme, Big Tree, who was known to have executed whites by chaining them to burning wagon wheels and scalping men alive, was released from prison in 1875 and eventually became a Sunday School teacher.

Towards Custer's Gold

'Gold from the grass roots down'

Throughout the 1860's, while the Comanches and Kiowas were fighting the army in the South, the war on the Northern Plains had continued to cause the army concern. Following the Civil War and Red Cloud's War, the white commanders had to reappraise how to tackle the problems posed by the Sioux and Cheyenne - the two most powerful tribes of the north. Before the Bozeman forts capitulated to Red Cloud's powerful stranglehold, the army attempted another offensive against the Indians in the area, concentrating its thrusts further south. This campaign has little connection with Red Cloud's War against Carrington. It was events during this encounter, christened 'Hancock's War', that introduced George Armstrong Custer to the hair-raising world of Indian fighting - an area where he initially excelled.

Long Hair

Custer was a Civil War hero, despite passing out of the West Point Military Academy bottom of his class with the most demerits ever. His astonishing rise to the rank of brigadier general by the age of 23 earned him the epithet 'The Boy General', which somewhat rankled with his peers. He was even present at the signing of Lee's surrender at Appomattox on 9 April 1865. In appreciation for his good work, Custer received a gift from General Sheridan - the table on which the cease-fire was signed. But after the war Custer was restless. He was sent to Texas and by the beginning of 1866 he lost his peacetime 'token rank' of major general. An opportunity for action came with the formation of the 7th Cavalry in June 1866. He was assigned to it as a lieutenant colonel and posted to Fort Riley in Kansas. Custer first led the 7th Cavalry in action in 1867, as part of Hancock's Campaign. 1867 wasn't a particularly good year for campaigns and Major General Hancock achieved little, though Custer did most damage. After Hancock razed a deserted village, the Indians declared war and Custer was despatched to run them down. Custer was christened 'Pahuska' (Long Hair) by the Indians because of his distinctive blond locks. During the chase the crafty Indians played cat and mouse with Custer and his frontier inexperience showed through. Custer operated out of Forts Hayes, McPherson and Wallace and gave his superiors much to worry about. On one occasion he sent an undermanned wagon train to Fort Wallace, which was attacked by Indians. On another he desperately wanted to visit his wife

Elizabeth (whom he always referred to as 'Libby') in Fort Riley, 150 miles away. This unnecessary mercy dash led to Custer being court-martialled and suspended without rank or pay for twelve months.

The Forsyth Saga

Hancock's ineptitude eventually became an embarrassment and he was relieved, leaving the army with more explaining to do to the government. General Sheridan replaced Hancock and came up with an innovative idea. Since the Indians didn't fight in the winter, that was when the army would attack them. If the army had cried 'foul' when Hancock burned down a deserted village, surely a winter campaign was even more underhand. The new offensive did offer one innovation. The officer chosen by Sheridan to lead the campaign was another Civil War hero - Major Forsyth. Forsyth maintained that if the Indian war parties were constantly harassed, they wouldn't be able to hunt for food, in addition to raiding homesteads and stagecoaches (especially in the run up to wintertime). Sheridan agreed and allowed Forsyth to form a small flying column of 50 seasoned Civil War veterans - crack marksmen one and all. They were the equivalent of a large party of hardened scouts and consequently a formidable unit. Their supplies were spartan, carried on four pack mules (supply wagons were one of the reasons conventional campaigning was so slow). For defence each man packed a Colt revolver and a seven-shot Spencer repeating rifle. An attack nearby, resulting in the deaths of two teamsters, allowed Forsyth to try out their effectiveness. The troops rode out of Fort Wallace on 6 September 1868, into Colorado, on the trail of a large band of raiders. Forsyth's lieutenant was another Civil War veteran named Beecher. By the 16 September they had reached the Arikara Fork of the Republican River, where they made camp. Early signs had shown that the group of Indians ahead was pretty big, possibly too much for the small pursuing party. One of the party, Louis McLoughlin noted later, "We knew for two days that we were biting off a chew that we couldn't get away with." In fact, the Sioux, Cheyenne and Arapaho camp was only 12 miles upriver and they knew the troops were approaching.

Convinced that his quarry was running away and that he still had the element of surprise, Forsyth rested his men for the night. But at dawn on the 17 September, about 600 Indians, under Tall Bull and Pawnee Killer, attacked Forsyth's bivouac. As the Indians struck, Forsyth made a crucial decision. He shifted his position from the riverbank and set up a defence in the shallows, on a sandy island roughly 20 by 60 yards. The first charge, led by Tall Bull, looked like it would overwhelm the defenders but Forsyth made his superior firepower count. Defending their shallow firing pits scooped out of the sand, the soldiers let rip with fearsome volleys. The Indians, their charge already slowed down by galloping through the water, couldn't withstand the barrage and broke. Forsyth was wounded in this first action, while his sidekick Beecher was killed. The Indians assaulted again and again throughout the day, beating war drums and blowing whistles. But to no avail - they couldn't break the soldiers' makeshift defence. The Indians were buoyed by the arrival of their great war chief Roman Nose. Roman Nose hadn't been involved in the fight up to that point because he was convinced that he would be killed if he went to war that day. In the event, he should have stayed at home. Accused of cowardice, Roman Nose led the next charge, even though he hadn't performed his habitual medicine rites on his war bonnet. The Indians charged and this time their progress wasn't slowed by the constant rifle fire. They were upon the soldiers' position when one of the soldiers shot Roman Nose at point-blank range. The charge broke, Roman Nose was mortally wounded and the Indians retreated to lick their wounds (and bury Roman Nose).

The following day the Indians didn't attack, choosing instead to make sure the soldiers stayed put. So far Forsyth had lost 7 men, with many more wounded. Forsyth realised they were in a tight spot. The Indians were going to starve them out. Forsyth had already decided to try and get help from Fort Wallace, 100 miles away. Two of the uninjured, a trapper and a trooper, had departed under cover of darkness on a seemingly impossible mission. Meanwhile, throughout the day the heat took a terrible toll, especially on the wounded, while the dead began to reek. On the third day of the siege, the Indians still didn't try an all-out attack, but kept the troops pinned down with rifle fire. The fourth day was more of the same and on the fifth the soldiers began to eat their own horses, while two more messengers were sent. On the eighth day, with a grisly end in sight for the weary, near-starved defenders, a column of the 10th Cavalry arrived and broke the siege. All four messengers had got through to Fort Wallace and Forsyth was saved. Remarkably he had lost only 7 dead, but over twenty of his men were wounded. The relief column found Forsyth slumped in his foxhole, calmly reading a copy of Dickens' 'Oliver Twist.' The men's horses had been their saviours - first as mounts, then as barricades and finally as supper. The glorious encounter (which attained near-mythical stature across the West) was named The Battle of Beecher's Island in honour of the young lieutenant who perished in the fighting. It is also known as the Battle of the Arikara (the site of the battle) and the Fight Where Roman Nose Was Killed (by the Indians, for obvious reasons).

Washita River

The failure of Forsyth's innovative idea led to an abandonment of the streamlined 'flying column' tactic as the army resumed more conventional campaign techniques. Since the Hancock debacle, Custer had been ignored for active service, but he was called back for Sheridan's winter campaign following the Forsyth saga. He was again stationed in Kansas and marched out against bands of Indians who had been raiding local settlements. The savages had attacked throughout the summer of 1868 and had mingled with 'peaceful' bands for the winter, hoping to avoid punishment. On 26 November Chief Black Kettle (of Sand Creek fame) and other Indian delegates had met with a white peace council. Again the Indians had been told their villages, now located on the Washita River, were safe for the winter. But this time the whites present were fully aware of Sheridan's upcoming plans - almost immediately there would be a campaign against the Cheyenne. Any Indians not compliant with the army must be sought out and either killed or captured. Custer left Fort Dodge with 800 men and rested at Camp Supply. He set off from there on 23 November, following the raiders' trail with a brief to seek and destroy. Three days later the column discovered that the trail led to Black Kettle's Washita camp. At dawn on the 27 November, to the strains of the cavalry band playing the ditty 'Garryowen', the troops swept into the village unannounced and began killing, in a terrible rerun of the Sand Creek Massacre. This time there was one crucial difference. Black Kettle and his wife were killed, along with 103 of his people, though only 11 of them were warriors. Custer captured the camp very easily and was in the process of moving on to the next one when he realised that help was arriving for the hostiles from the surrounding camps. Instead of pressing his advantage (which he would lose completely if he was outnumbered) Custer retreated, but not before torching Black Kettle's camp, killing nearly 900 Indian horses and releasing his 50 women and children captives (they would slow him down too much). His actions were highly commended by Sheridan. The operation was a novelty for the general - it actually achieved something. But Custer's tactics were remarkably close to Chivington's at Sand Creek.

The moral argument this time wasn't establishing whether these Cheyenne were 'definitely warlike.' The one real problem most people had with the Battle of Washita River was the fate of Major Elliot and his 19-man reconnaissance party. The previous evening it was Elliot's group who had found the Indian village. During the action on 27 November, Custer had dispatched him in pursuit of the routed Indians, but because of the unexpected arrival of the Indian reinforcements, Custer had been forced to withdraw without the major. Other members of Custer's command wanted to go and search for Elliot, but Custer flatly refused. Weeks later the corpses of Elliot's party were discovered a little way from the Washita site. They had been cut-off and massacred by Arapahos riding from a nearby camp to aid Black Kettle. True, Custer couldn't risk his whole command for the sake of the few, but it was his duty to help members of his own command in peril. As it turned out, several cavalry officers never forgave Custer for his 'cowardice', though the Washita victory was touted as a great success for the army and it certainly put paid to notions of a quiet winter for the Indians. In a short time various bands of Cheyenne, Arapaho and Comanches began to drift into custody at Fort Cobb - their stores of food burned, their hunting horses killed and their homes in ruins. It was a hard way to win a war, but Sheridan was a ruthless man.

Gold In Them There Hills!

In the Powder River country, the Bozeman Trail forts had been burned down and Red Cloud had won a great victory. The white invasion had been slowed, perhaps even stopped altogether. But the government's plans for a new railroad in Yellowstone country went ahead. Custer stayed in Kansas for a couple more years and was then sent to Kentucky, a side-step in terms of his military career. He spent his time fighting the Ku Klux Klan, which was at least more worthy than killing Indians. But Custer was in love with the romance and adventure of Indian fighting, and he was soon back on the frontier. In 1873 he was posted to North Dakota - his 7th Cavalry would protect the railroad survey parties mapping the Yellowstone River area (about 100 miles north of the site of Fort Phil Kearny and the Big Horn Mountains). It was there that Custer first encountered a man who would turn out to be his chief nemesis - the Oglala Sioux Crazy Horse. The survey team left Fort Rice in June 1873, with an escort of Custer's cavalry and a large party of infantry, led by General Stanley, a heavy drinker. The surveying went well, but the column was constantly harassed by war parties led by Crazy Horse. In one encounter, Custer showed uncharacteristic caution and didn't walk headlong into a well-laid (and potentially fatal) ambush. But the mapping foray was for nought, as the Northern Pacific Railroad went bust shortly after the expedition returned.

Custer had acquitted himself well and the following year he was given a similar assignment - except that this time the outcome would have far more sinister repercussions. In the summer of 1874 a column under Custer was despatched to the Black Hills of Dakota. Their purpose was to confirm the countrywide rumours that the area contained gold deposits, just waiting to be found. The motives behind such a foray were the subject of much subterfuge. There was no railroad about to pass through the area, so a survey party couldn't trespass. Instead the government claimed that they were scouting for the site of a new army stockade. But probably more than anything, the government wanted a large-scale invasion of Indian land by whites - to stir up trouble - and then send troops there to quell the massacres. The problem was, according to the Fort Laramie Treaty of 1868, the Black Hills belonged to the Sioux. The land was lush, well-stocked with nature's larder and the whites wanted it for themselves. Only the Indians stood in their way. A stampede of prospectors would give the government the perfect excuse, as they often had no control over the grizzled rabble who called themselves 'Forty-niners.' That Custer, whether knowingly or not, participated in this plan is crucially important. It was his expedition into the Black Hills (an area the Indians held sacred) that precipitated the most famous Indian War and led to the battle that resulted in Custer's death. In 1874, Custer was stationed at Fort Abraham Lincoln (on the Missouri River) and it was from there that his 1200 strong 'fort survey' party departed on 2 July. Included in the personnel were some suspicious additions - two prospectors and three journalists. They headed west and then turned south, blazing a trail into the Black Hills that the Indians would come to call the 'Thieves Road.' At the end of the 'Thieves Road' Custer found gold at French Creek. Sources vary as to how much he found. Some say the quantities were hardly worth mentioning, while others described mountains hewn of it. Custer's official reports predictably opted for the latter and newspaper headlines soon boasted that the Black Hills were loaded with 'Gold From The Grass Roots Down.' One publication subtly opined, 'The National Debt To Be Paid When Custer Returns.' Custer was again the nation's hero. He had proved an age-old myth and found gold in the hills. It was fairy tale stuff, his own El Dorado. The entire area was inundated with prospectors, settlers and assorted riffraff - in the very midst of the sacred heartland of the Indians. These interlopers raped the land (killing game, cutting timber, scaring buffalo) and with it the Indian nation. If the Sioux and Cheyenne had hated Custer after Washita, their hatred was now tenfold. Thereafter Custer got a new name from the Indians - 'Chief of All Thieves.' It suited him.

A Good Day To Die

'One does not sell the earth on which the people walk'

In 1868, in the weeks following the burning of the Bozeman forts, the victorious Indians met white delegates at Laramie. But many Indians passed on the chance for peace. Crazy Horse of the Oglala Sioux (who had been instrumental in Red Cloud's victories) refused to attend and so too did Sitting Bull of the Hunkpapa branch of the Sioux. Instead, as Indians who epitomised the spirit of freedom amongst their people (and for their bravery), they were bestowed with the honour of chieftainship of their respective bands. From this point these two men - demonstrating power, charisma and cunning - were the Sioux Nation's best chance of defeating the whitemen. They also planned and executed the most famous victory against the army during the entire Indian Wars and robbed America of a national hero. America would never forgive them.

Sitting Bull

Probably the most famous Indian leader of all was Sitting Bull - chief, prophet and mystic of the Hunkpapa Sioux. The Hunkpapa were one of seven tribes that made up the Lakota or Teton Sioux, who lived in the west of Dakota. The eastern branch was the Santee Sioux, who had been the perpetrators of the Minnesota Massacre in 1862. The other six branches of the Lakota were the Miniconjou, the Brulé, the Sans Arc, the Oohenonpa, the Oglala and the Sihasapa. Each band's name meant something different. Hunkpapa meant 'Those Who Camp By The Entrance' (i.e. the entrance to the camp). Sitting Bull was born in 1831 (some sources say 1834) and was originally named 'Slow.' During a raid on their enemies the Crows, Slow counted coup in the melee and thereafter his father Returns Again renamed him Tananka Iyotake or Sitting Bull Buffalo (shortened to Sitting Bull). As he rose to prominence among the tribe he became well known as a peacemaker and visionary, but also as a fearsome fighter. Although he fought against the whites throughout the 1860's, he also led raids on their warlike neighbours, especially the Crows. But it was the arrival of the white man that assured Sitting Bull a place in history. In one celebrated incident in 1872, Sitting Bull proved to his compatriots that he was almost invincible. It was during the railway-surveying mission on the Yellowstone, when Sitting Bull was involved in a skirmish with the army. While a large party of Sioux attacked a group of soldiers escorting the surveyors, Sitting Bull sat down during the action and smoked a pipe, completely oblivious to the hail of bullets. Was it an act of bravery, a reckless gesture of defiance or a rather graphic (and extremely dangerous) way of advocating peace? Whatever, it was good medicine for the Sioux, who saw him as a strong leader in their forthcoming struggle with the whites.

Crazy Horse

His ally in the fight against the whites was a chief named Crazy Horse of the Oglala. The Oglala (meaning 'Those Who Scatter Their Own') were like the Hunkpapa and often quarrelled with their neighbours. These feuds revolved around the usual reasons, ranging from hunting rights and horse stealing, to insults and petty bickering. Their nomadic existence meant that they were constantly on the move and in the process they dislodged other bands from the Black Hills area. Before the whites proved to be a problem, the Sioux had forced the Kiowas further south and edged the Crows further north. The Crows never forgot this and later scouted for the army to defeat their old enemies, failing to realise the wider implications of their help. Another tribe, the Cheyenne, were also enemies of the Sioux, but they became strong allies in 1843 and would remain so until the aftermath of the Sioux War. Crazy Horse was born in 1841 and his birth name was 'Curly' because of his curly hair. Curly's father was a holy man named Crazy Horse (or Tashunka Witko in Sioux). As was often the Indian custom, when Curly came of age he inherited his father's name, while his father was lumbered with a poor replacement - 'Worm.' Crazy Horse Junior's acts of daring occurred fighting Arapahos, but he happily joined the war against the whites in 1865, in the aftermath of the Sand Creek Massacre. Crazy Horse was involved in many of the key engagements of the Indian Wars and his exploits were of such outlandish bravery as to seem foolhardy. He was present at the brutal Battle of the River Platte, the first post-Civil War engagement of the Indian Wars. On 25 July 1865 3000 Sioux, Cheyenne and Arapahos attacked a makeshift army stockade at the Platte River station. The station guarded a bridge across the Platte (on the California-Oregon Trail), but the Indians saw the span as a symbol of white encroachment into their lands. Indian decoys tried to draw the soldiers out of the fort, but they failed and reinforcements managed to reach the stockade to bolster the command. On the following day the troops did emerge, but not to confront the decoys. They had spotted a wagon train approaching and were riding to protect it. The Indians, led by Roman Nose, attacked in force and cut off the wagons and the relief force. In a heated engagement the Indians encircled the wagons. After a protracted four-hour siege they burned the freight, killed the whites and tortured the wounded in front of their comrades at the fort. Crazy Horse was subsequently prominent in Red Cloud's War and took part in the Fetterman Massacre, the Wagon Box Fight and the burning of Fort C F Smith (following its evacuation in 1868). Throughout these encounters Crazy Horse's speciality was commanding the Indian decoys, with the intention of luring the soldiers into a false sense of security and hopefully to their deaths. Put simply, Crazy Horse was the bait for Red Cloud's trap. Soon he would help to bait the biggest trap of all.

Black Gold

Following the discovery of gold in the Black Hills (or 'Ha Sapa' as the Indians called them), the area was swarming with prospectors throughout the summer of 1875. In an irrational moment, the peace council had assured the Indians (during the Laramie Treaty of 1868) that the Black Hills would be theirs indefinitely. The government could see the huge blunder the council had made and set about removing the Indians from the land. As one newspaper of the time saw it - 'What shall be done with these Indian dogs in our manger? They will not dig the gold or let others do it.' The Indians saw absolutely no value in the yellow metal and couldn't understand the whites' fascination with the stuff. The sacred landscape was far more precious to them than gold and they refused to let the army bully them out of the hills. The government decided that they would buy the Black Hills from the Indians - as though the rightful owners could put a financial value on their birthright. There was no such problem for the government, but this deal was going to cost them more than a few beads and some antique rifles. They offered Red Cloud $6,000,000 for the Black Hills, or $400,000 (per annum) for the mining rights. After a brief confab, the Indian leaders vetoed both proposals. What were they going to do with $6,000,000? The Black Hills contained all the wealth they needed, certainly enough to sustain their simple lifestyle. Indians didn't have a complete grasp of financial matters anyway. Red Cloud had initially asked for the astronomical sum of $600,000,000. In the event, the government were told, "No sale."

With so many whites in the area (1000 by the summer of 1875), something had to be done. Not only were the prospectors illegally trespassing, their lives were at risk from retaliation from incensed Sioux. President Grant went for the immoderate option. He issued a proclamation that all Indians who didn't move from the area in question (including the Black Hills and the Powder River country) would be treated as antagonists and rounded up into reservations. The statement was unequivocal - all Indians who didn't surrender were hostile. The deadline for their surrender was 31

January 1876, which happened to be the middle of winter. It was well known to the government that the Indians didn't move much in the winter months. They abandoned their nomadic existence, chose a spot to set up camp and stayed there. It was a time of recuperation, as they lived in virtual hibernation - living off their stores of food gathered throughout the autumn.

The winter of 1875-76 was terrible and some of the couriers taking the ultimatum to the Indian camps couldn't reach their destination or got snowed in. The Indians were either unwilling to move or never received their messages. None came into the reservations and the deadline passed. Perhaps the winter deadline was a deliberate ploy by the government to force a confrontation. Previously the politicians had had little luck stopping the whites trespassing on Indian land. To their credit, the army had initially tried to stem the flow of prospectors in the area (sometimes burning their wagons and turning them back) but there were simply too many. Newspapers fuelled the pro-mining sentiment and turned against the army, with unhelpful comments like, 'If there is gold in the Black Hills, no army on earth can keep the adventurous men of the west out of them.' Moreover, the prospecting camps rapidly grew to good-sized settlements, which quickly metamorphosed into bustling towns. Deadwood was the prime example - a town completely dependent on the gold mining operations in the area. So it was decided that it would be easier to shift the Indians. The army riding into the mining settlements and turfing white squatters out wouldn't go down very well with the eastern press. Putting the hostiles in their place (i.e. on government-run reservations) would.

The man for the job was Custer. His experience was perfect for such a mission and it would also be poetic justice. He had discovered the gold and would now evict the Indians, so that the Gold Rush could begin in earnest. Not everyone was unanimous in their praise of the 7th Cavalry's commander, but no one could deny that he had an aura that made him a charismatic figure. His detractors argued that his methods were inhumane. Custer had a proven track record of glory-seeking, recklessness and irresponsibility - needlessly risking the lives of his men and wantonly killing Indian women and children, though his superiors saw these as boons in a winter campaign. With half an eye on a political career, this momentous push into Sioux country (in Centennial Year no less) would be the icing on the cake for Custer, the army's most flamboyant character and a national hero. But Sheridan's plans were dashed. Unfortunately Custer was unavailable - he had to testify before a congressional committee about fraudulent dealings by Indian traders. General Crook (the old Apache Indian fighter) filled in for Custer and led the first offensive. By March the Northern Indian bands were starting to form one large tribe. The troops must strike soon or there would be too many Indians to fight.

So on 1 March 1876, Crook led a column out of Fort Fetterman and headed up the Bozeman Trail, hoping that the name of the fort didn't have any bearing on the outcome of his campaign. Riding through appalling conditions, including severe snowdrifts, Crook knew the villages were near, having found a trail on the evening of 16 March. Putting Sheridan's winter tactics into operation, he sent Colonel Reynolds with 300 men on a recce. A smaller group would have a better chance of surprising the hostiles. On the 17 March, Reynolds found a large Cheyenne village on the banks of the Tongue River. Surmising they had caught the camp unawares, Reynolds further divided his force and sent 50 of his men into the sleeping camp to destroy it. Though the attack was a moderate success (the Indians' ponies and supplies were captured), the troops were unable to press home their advantage and most of the Cheyenne escaped. Sources vary as to whose camp it was - some say it belonged to Two Moons, others say Old Bear or Little Wolf. They're all correct, as all three Cheyenne leaders were present, though the army's claim that the village sheltered Crazy Horse was erroneous. Because of the appalling weather (which hit minus 40°) the campaign faltered and the troops withdrew, while the Indians managed to recapture many of their horses. The strike was deemed a failure by Sheridan, who was unhappy with Crook's tactics. It was decided that a more concentrated campaign would be needed during the summer.

Ironically the Cheyenne villagers attacked were on their way to a reservation for the winter, but the attack convinced them otherwise. If they weren't aggressive before, they certainly were now. One of the leaders, Short Bull, claimed that if it hadn't been for the attack by Crook, there wouldn't have been a Sioux War, but the suggestion seems fanciful, as both sides were geared up for a fight. Scouts had reported that the Indians had been stockpiling arms and ammunition for months - something was definitely afoot. By summer thousands of Indians had gathered in the Rosebud Valley, Montana. There were warriors from many tribes of the Northern Plains - the Hunkpapa, Oglala, Miniconjou, Brulé and Sans Arcs plus groups of Arapahos and Cheyenne. Amongst their leaders were Crazy Horse, Spotted Eagle, Gall, Rain In the Face and Two Moon. This huge force was united by Sitting Bull. It was he who had prophesied the forthcoming battle. During a Sun Dance ceremony in June, Sitting Bull had 100 pieces of flesh stripped from his arms. In a trance-like state he saw soldiers falling from the sky into their huge camp. It was a good omen.

Battle On The Rosebud

The new campaign was better organised than before. It involved a three-pronged strike force. In the south, Crook again left Fort Fetterman with 1000 men. In the west was Colonel Gibbon's force of 500 men out of Fort Ellis. In the east was Brigadier General Terry from Fort Abraham Lincoln. Included in this 900-man column was Custer's Seventh Cavalry (about 600 strong). Hopefully the Indians would be caught between this trinity and destroyed. Custer had missed the first part of the show and had vowed to be around for the finale. But like Crook's strike that March, Custer was over-looked for the summer campaign and he ended up literally begging Terry to take him along. It would prove to be a fateful decision.

It was Crook who drew first blood in the Sioux War of 1876. He headed northwest from Fort Fetterman and set up a base camp at Goose Creek, to the southeast of the main Indian forces. Crook's 1000 strong force (of which a fifth were infantry) had been augmented with about 250 Indian auxiliaries. On 14 June, Crook was joined by 170 Crow warriors (under Chief Old Crow) and 80 Shoshonis (under Chief Washakie, an avid supporter of the whites). These expert horsemen would be excellent allies, as there was no love lost between either tribe and the Sioux. The army played on these tribal differences and encouraged the Crows and Shoshonis to join them in the forthcoming campaign. The warriors, looking for a chance to get revenge on their old enemies, obliged. Crook ventured forth and was soon moving into the heart of Sioux country. He made camp on the Rosebud River on June 16, but he had been spotted by a party of Cheyenne hunters. It was there, on the morning of 17 June, that Crazy Horse and about 2,000 warriors attacked Crook's army. The Indians took the troops by surprise, but Crook's Indian allies managed to repulse the initial attack and allow Crook time to organise his forces. Even so, his tactical ineptitude almost led to disaster. Having rallied his men and seemingly stemmed the Indian attack, Crook ordered Captain Mills and his cavalry to withdraw from the battle and attack Crazy Horse's village, which he presumed was nearby. But Crook was wrong and instead of trying to waylay Mills, Crazy Horse, using a pocket mirror to give his forces commands, concentrated his attack on the point Mills had left undermanned. Luckily Mills had the fore-sight to see that his assignment wasn't going to have any bearing on the battle and turned back, inadvertently outflanking the hostiles and forcing them to flee. It was during this battle that Crazy Horse uttered his famous battle cry, "Today is a good day to fight, today is a good day to die", which is often mistakenly attributed to the Battle of the Little Big Horn - perhaps he said it twice. Crook had won the Battle of the Rosebud, but only by good fortune - the Crows and Shoshonis had fought tenaciously, while Mills' return had saved the day. That said, it was a hollow victory as Crook's force was in disarray. He didn't have the resources to continue the summer campaign and so headed back to base camp. This immediately threw a spanner into Terry's three-pronged master plan. One column had not only been delayed, but had been taken out of the equation altogether.

The Cunning Plan

Meanwhile in the north, Terry, Gibbon and Custer rendezvoused on 21 June on the Yellowstone River. There, aboard the supply steamer 'Far West', Terry outlined his strategy to his field officers. They were aware that the Indians were in the general area of the offensive, but not of their exact position. Major Reno, from Custer's command, had been scouting and found a camp trail in the Big Horn region, signifying the presence of hostiles. Terry's plan was simple enough - a variation of the campaigns that had preceded it, but now involving many more troops in a pincer movement. Gibbon and Custer would move two separate columns into hostile territory. Custer would try to flush out the Indians and Gibbon and/or Crook would block their escape, depending on whether the Indians ran north or south. The crucial part was that Custer mustn't attack before 26 June, by which time Gibbon would be in position. Any breach of this order could have severe ramifications and upset the balance of the plan. To entrust such a delicate, carefully laid strategy to an arrogant, headstrong officer like Custer was a questionable course of action. Seasoned officers could have told Terry that Custer would probably not bother to follow his orders to the letter, especially where fellow officers were concerned. He was never one to share the credit for anything. Following the Battle of the Rosebud, the Indians had indeed been active in the Big Horn region, shifting their camp from the Rosebud to the Big Horn Valley. They made camp there on the night of the 23 June, in an area they called the 'Greasy Grass.' Taking the maxim 'safety in numbers' to the extreme, the camp contained about 10,000 people, including between 3000 and 4000 warriors. It was the largest Indian war party ever assembled. If Custer was thinking of a repeat of his attack on the Washita River camp, he was in for a big surprise.

The Indians, displaying total assurance in their vast force, simply waited to see the army's next move. Little did the army know that their plan was already off the rails. The 'Far West' meeting knew nothing of Crook's run-in with Crazy Horse. There would be no attack on two fronts. The whole Indian force would be able to concentrate on Custer and Gibbon. Before he left, Custer refused the offer of extra troops from Terry's command, including some men from the 2nd Cavalry and a battery of Gatling guns. Much has been made of this decision. Though the troops would have been handy, Gatling guns were unreliable weapons. On form they were lethal, but overheating and other problems blighted their effectiveness on the frontier. So it was that Custer and the 7th Cavalry rode out at noon on 22 June 1876. The contingent was something of a family outing for the Custer family. Custer's brother Captain Tom Custer commanded Troop C of the Seventh. Another of his brothers, Boston, was a civilian forage master with the regiment. Lieutenant Calhoun, L Troop's commanding officer, was Custer's brother-in-law, while Armstrong Reed, a civilian guest, was Custer's nephew. Custer's two subordinates were Major Reno, an excellent Civil War veteran with little frontier experience, and Captain Benteen, who hated Custer's guts after Major Elliot's betrayal at Washita. Custer proceeded south, as per the plan, and began to follow the trail Reno had discovered earlier that week along the Rosebud. It was not a difficult trail to follow - Reno would have had to have been blind to have missed it. It was half a mile wide and consisted of a powdery dust, with deep grooves made by the Indians' travois. Along the route there were abandoned campsites, littered with the debris of camp life - animal carcasses, blankets, morsels of food and campfires. Ominously, the embers in the fires were getting warmer and warmer, the further down the trail Custer went. Pretty soon they'd be red-hot.

Custer hurried his men along the trail and seemed to have totally forgotten Terry's plan. He was supposed to ride south, then turn north to cut off the Indians' escape route from Gibbon's assault. But he continued to follow the Indian camp trail as it arced west towards the Big Horn River. The signs got worse and the Arikara and Crow Indian scouts who rode with Custer started to get nervous. Everything they saw pointed to disaster. One thing was sure, the Sioux and their allies weren't afraid to be found. That alone unnerved the scouts. Even more frightening was the size of the trail. The huge numbers of Indians involved told the scouts what they were up against. They tried to get through to Custer, but their commander was adamant. He knew that if he attacked this immense village he would be a hero. His scouts knew if he attacked the immense village, they would be dead. As soon as Custer deviated from Terry's plan, he took a risk. But all the signs now pointed to a group of Indians the soldiers couldn't handle. Custer ordered a night march on 24 June, which gained precious time, but sapped the energy of his men. Ahead of the column rode Lieutenant Varnum and some scouts, who made the most disturbing discovery of all. On the morning of Sunday 25 June 1876, from a vantage point called the Crow's Nest, the scouts saw something they had never seen in their lives - in the distance, maybe 20 miles away, the hills seemed to be moving. Then it dawned on the scouts. The moving landscape wasn't land at all, but thousands of horses - the biggest horse herd they had ever seen, about 20,000 animals in total. The implications of such a huge herd were considerably more worrying than the trail.

Later that morning, Custer and the rest of the column caught up with Varnum at the Crow's Nest. Custer couldn't see the horses, nor the village beyond, even though his eagle-eyed scouts insisted it was there - "Many Indians", said the Crows, "Big village." By now Custer's force was about 12 miles to the southeast of the Indian village, near a river called Ash Creek. While Custer's troops were resting up, the scouts spotted a group of Indians riding down the Big Horn River, away from the soldiers. Two things struck Varnum - the Indians were about to raise the alarm and possibly even run away without a fight. Neither assumption was true. The Indians had known for several days that Custer was in the area (their scouts were excellent too) and the Indians weren't running away, but riding to the village to get ready for the fight. Varnum immediately told Custer that the Indians were on the move. Custer quickly decided to split his force and (theoretically) take the Indians by surprise, by attacking their village. He divided his force into four groups. He sent Captain Benteen, with 125 men (three cavalry companies - H, D and K), to swing west and scout for hostiles. Then he sent Reno up Ash Creek (again with 125 men, troops A, G and M plus most of the scouts), towards the Big Horn to attack the village from the south. When Reno hit the village, Custer would support Reno's assault with his force. This consisted of five cavalry troops (C, E, F, I and L) - 215 men all told, plus 13 officers, 3 scouts, a surgeon and 5 civilians. The fourth group (a single company of troopers) brought up the rear with the pack mules and supplies. The companies parted at just past noon, with Benteen receiving his orders and setting off without knowing that Custer had further weakened his force by giving Reno a separate assignment. Moreover, as Reno set off across the Ash Creek ford, Custer didn't follow him (as Reno had assumed), but instead stayed on the other bank and rode out of sight, into the hills. Custer was obviously using Reno as a decoy, to draw the Indians out, while he hit the village from another angle.

Time was of the essence and Reno set a fast pace as he headed for the village. It took him about three hours to get within striking distance, finally crossing the Little Big Horn River. Once in the valley, Reno formed his men into a battle line and charged on the encampment. Custer had attacked Black Kettle's camp on Washita River with a command of 800 men. Reno was about to attack a vastly superior camp with a force a fraction of the size. Reno didn't stand a chance. As they approached, Reno's command was met by a huge force of about 700 Indians led by war chief Gall. For whatever reason, upon seeing this mass of warriors, Reno halted his men, dismounted and formed a skirmish line to meet the attack. But soon, with the Indians attacking in overwhelming numbers, Reno was forced to retreat to a small wood. There he could wait for Custer's arrival and launch another attack on the village. He was going to have a long wait. The Indians set about flushing Reno from the wood and set fire to the undergrowth. Panicking, Reno decided that it would be better to avoid being completely surrounded in the trees and to make a break for the high ground on the other side of the Little Big Horn River. Confusion reigned as Reno tried to get his men to safety. Some carried on fighting, others didn't hear the order to retreat. As the main force broke cover and made the mile-long dash for the river, many wounded men were left behind to the mercy of the Sioux. Even in the open country, the Indians were far superior riders and galloped alongside the soldiers, killing them at will. Finally Reno managed to get across the river and occupy the hills on the other side, but he'd lost a lot of men - over 35 dead and many wounded and missing. But strangely the Indians didn't continue to attack. A few kept Reno occupied, while the majority rode north, back towards the village. Then in the distance, Reno's men could hear gunfire. Reno's command was in bad shape and he was in no fit state to reprise his attack on the village. The soldiers could only wait helplessly for the outcome of the faraway battle.

Battle Of The Little Big Horn

When Reno set off, Custer had taken a roughly parallel northeasterly route, on the other side of Ash Creek, concealing his position by keeping low behind the hills. After a couple of hours, Custer rode to the top of the ridge to see what was beyond. It was from here that he saw the middle section of the vast Indian village stretching down the valley beyond. But what he was seeing was only part of the camp because it wound into the distance and was partially obscured by the topography. As far as Custer was concerned it was Washita all over again. "We've got them", Custer told his men, "We've caught them napping." He immediately sent a message to Benteen with Sergeant Butler, urging him to hurry with the extra supply train. Now Custer pressed on towards the camp. Finally, before he turned down from the hills towards the ford that would take him straight into the village, Custer sent bugler Giovanni Martini (sometimes anglicised as 'John Martin') to Benteen with another plea. It read: 'Benteen. Come on. Big village. Be quick. Brings packs'. Martini rode off, but as he looked back he saw Indians appearing on either side of Custer's column, as they approached the ford via a ravine. It was about 3pm - at about the same time Reno was sheltering in the timber, after hitting the southern end of the village. Whatever happened next, Martini was the last white to ride out of the valley alive.

There is no definitive version of how Custer attacked the camp and several sources proffer different theories. The most widely believed version states that Custer rode out of the hills towards the Miniconjou Ford and panic (or perhaps celebration, in view of Sitting Bull's prediction) broke out in the village. A large number of the Indians were further south, mauling Reno, but the camp was by no means undefended. As soon as Custer appeared, Crazy Horse and the other war chiefs put their plan, an immense trap, into operation. A few braves (probably no more than a dozen) harassed Custer as he approached. This was the encounter Martini saw as he rode to Benteen. But soon the dozen became hundreds as battle proper began. Initially the encounter resembled Reno's aborted attack. Custer headed for the ford, to hit the village, but sheer weight of numbers turned him back. Naturally he made for the high ground, as he saw the massive force emerging from the village. Custer fell back to the northeast, with the Indians pressing all the time. There the troops took up a defensive position. Troop L and I covered their rear, Troops E, F and C were the vanguard. Having repulsed Reno's men, Gall and his men careered back through the village, across the ford Custer tried to use and straight into Troops I and L. They pushed Custer further and further up the hill, picking off the soldiers with arrows and rifles, before rushing in for hand-to-hand combat. The soldiers fought bravely but there was nothing they could do against such numbers. In addition, the heat of the June afternoon was torturous, the dust and smoke choking. Conventional tactics meant nothing in such circumstances. One Indian eyewitness said that some of the soldiers panicked, threw away their weapons and pleaded for mercy, while another Indian watching from the village said the battle was just a huge cloud of dust, out of which emerged riderless cavalry horses.

Dismounted, the troops tried to huddle in any cover they could find or behind their steeds' corpses in an improvised defence, but they were being driven back all the time. The Indians attacked ferociously in waves, on horseback and on foot, alternately charging, then stopping to whittle down the troopers with rifle fire. In one instance it seems that a 15-man skirmish line from Troop I was felled in a single concentrated volley from a group of Indian snipers hidden in some bushes nearby. The rearguard Troops went first, leaving the vanguard to form a pitiful cluster in a last stand against the onslaught. While the troops made their way as best they could to the top of the ridge, there was one final surprise in store. On the other slope Crazy

Horse, with hundreds of warriors, was roaring up the other side. Custer never reached the summit. As the soldiers ran out of ammunition (most of which was in the saddlebags of horses that had long since stampeded), the Indians rushed in, killing them all. It is generally believed that Custer was one of the last to be killed on the hill. But it seems the finale of the battle wasn't Custer's Last Stand (as it has become known) atop the rise. One source states that a group of a dozen or so terrified men, who were pretending to be dead, suddenly got up and fled down the hill towards the ford, where they were cut down. Others say that some mounted men dashed for the river, but were similarly killed. The Indians casualties are not known, but range between 30 and 300. Several Indians claim to have killed Custer and the examination of his wounds merely shows that he died from one of two bullet wounds - one in the heart, one through the temple. He could even have shot himself, as the temple wound is consistent with such reasoning. Though there was evidence in the Indian camp that some white captives were taken from the battle and tortured later, many Indian participants say that everyone with Custer was killed immediately. The unlucky corpses in the village probably belonged to Reno's wounded, captured when they were left behind in the wood. There have also been several reports by charlatans claiming to be survivors from Custer's command (including the celebrated Crow scout Curly), but their tales have never been substantiated.

Centennial Celebration

The whole battle took about an hour, on the testimony of the soldiers with Reno, who heard the whole thing while helplessly sitting on their own hill two miles downstream. Benteen arrived at Reno's defence at about 4.30. He had been hurrying to help Custer (having received the 'Bring packs' message from Martini), but Reno implored him to stay. Benteen obliged, but a young officer, Captain Weir, couldn't believe fellow officers were leaving Custer to his fate. He took a company of men and went to a hill overlooking the valley. Benteen soon joined him. In the distance they could see the battlefield and many hundreds of warriors milling about, but no soldiers. Indians spotted the troops on the hill and moved against them, forcing Benteen and Weir back to Reno. There they were besieged for the night. On 26 June, the Indians renewed their attacks on the hill, keeping the soldiers pinned down. Many of Reno and Benteen's command went half crazy with thirst. But by afternoon the Indian firing subsided and at about 7pm, the whole encampment moved off south down the valley. They had won their great victory against Long Hair - Reno and Benteen didn't matter. There was also a much better reason to vacate the area. Terry and Gibbon's infantry column had been sighted in the vicinity and the Indians didn't want another fight. As the exodus moved into the distance, the Indian scouts with Reno couldn't understand why they could hear victory chants - what victory?

At dawn on 27 June, Reno could see that the campsite was empty and a dust cloud was approaching in the distance, so he sent 2 scouts out to meet what he hoped was the relief column. Meanwhile Terry rode through the abandoned village. There was the usual scatter of Indian detritus, but also some unusual and grisly finds - items of 7th Cavalry kit, funeral tepees containing dead braves, wounded cavalry mounts and several mangled white remains, including severed heads suspended from tent poles. The worst discovery was three detached heads, placed on the ground at points on a triangle, positioned facing each other in an eternal gaze. The relief column sent scouts to the east of the camp and soon found the site of the massacre. The bodies of 197 men were found and Terry was given the terrible news - it was Custer's outfit. Terry had received a sketchy report from some Crow scouts (who claimed to have been with Custer before the battle) that the command had been annihilated. Now he found it to be true. Having met Reno's messengers, Terry and Gibbon rode on to Reno's defensive position. It was only then that Reno and Benteen had their worst fears confirmed. While the wounded were tended, Terry's men set out to explore the battleground. First they traversed the river and the valley where Reno had fought. The white corpses strewn about were badly mutilated and covered in swarms of flies. Bodies were swiftly buried by the troops where they lay. The following day, the burial parties rode to the Custer battlefield. The site was covered with partially decomposed naked white bodies, nearly all mutilated and scalped. Some had been propped up and used as target practice for bowmen. Many had their hands, feet, noses, privates and heads severed. The wounded had been finished off by squaws with clubs. Troopers had been staked through the chest, had their eye sockets filled with arrows or their entrails removed. It was a terrible sight for their army comrades to see. Custer had been stripped naked except for his socks. According to official reports he wasn't scalped or mutilated, but had two bullet wounds. Unofficial reports state that he had his fingers cut off, awls pushed in his ears (the Indians said to make him 'hear better') and had been propped up on one elbow, to look like he was reclining - truly an eternal repose. The official report was probably concocted to comfort Custer's wife, Libby. Moreover, some reports state that Custer's body was found nowhere near the top of the 'Last Stand' hill (later renamed 'Custer Hill'), but much further down - insinuating that he died much earlier in the fight. Sergeant Butler was found dead a quarter of a mile from the battle. He was probably ambushed as he made his way to Benteen with Custer's first message. The soldiers buried the dead as best they could, in stony ground with few shovels. Rough wooden crosses marked the graves. Some of them read 'Unknown', the mutilations were so severe.

Later on 27 June, the column set off north, carrying the wounded on mule litters (essentially stretchers slung hammock-like between two animals). The wounded were then taken to the steamer 'Far West' and home for treatment. The able troopers camped on the mouth of the Big Horn River and awaited further orders. Slowly, the news leaked out about the massacre and soon it was common knowledge, with newspapers running the story nation-wide on 5 July 1876. The whole of America was mortified by the defeat and the press predictably looked for a scapegoat. The scapegoat's name was Reno. During an inquiry Reno was accused by his own officers and troops of cowardice and drunkenness. One witness claimed to have seen Reno down an entire bottle of whisky during the fight in the wood. But to call Reno a coward was very unfair. He didn't have a hope of reaching the village with his puny charge. Benteen was also targeted. He should have pressed on when he joined Reno. The inquiry's argument was that if Benteen had ridden to Custer's aid, the distraction might have given Custer a chance to escape. Both officers were exonerated, though their careers were irreparably damaged. Reno died in 1889, while Benteen was unrepentant, once saying of Custer, "I'm only too proud to say that I despised him." It was Custer, the man who couldn't be there to explain his actions, who was most to blame. He divided his command, risking everyone's lives. He charged into a village against obviously superior numbers and he disobeyed Terry's orders. It was his fault the plan went so disastrously awry and he paid the ultimate price. In so doing he became a martyr to the whites in their war with the Sioux. Sitting Bull and Crazy Horse had won their greatest victory and the summer campaign was in tatters - hardly the way the government would have liked to celebrate Centennial year. The exact details of events that summer's afternoon in Montana in 1876 will never be known, but the name Custer will forever be synonymous with folly and glory.

I Will Fight No More Forever

'The Great Spirit seemed to be looking the other way, and did
not see what was being done to my people'

One of the greatest stories of the Old West was the tale of the Nez Perce
and their famous leader, Chief Joseph. The Nez Perce were the most cul-
tured and resolute of all Indians, but to whitemen they were the same as
any other 'savage.' Seldom in the annals of American history did a tribe
make such a huge effort to live in peace with the whiteman and have their
efforts thwarted by ridiculous government measures and pig-headed generals, which resulted, ultimately, in tragedy.

The Pierced Noses

They were originally named the Chopunnish tribe by the first white
explorers to chart their stamping ground, in Idaho, Washington and Ore-
gon. But they were re-christened the Nez Percé by French trappers,
inspired by the Indians' shell nose-ornaments, worn as a primitive version
of body piercing. Over the years the name 'Nez Percé' lost the accent and
was anglicised to Nez Perce. In the fur trade wars of the late 1820's the Nez
Perce were initially allied to the British, but eventually sided with the
Americans, who for a time treated them as equals. Upon seeing the positive
effects of white mans' religion on some of their number, the Nez Perce
requested that missionaries should be despatched to teach them the ways of
the Lord. Among the Indians who entered into the Church of God (and
were baptised) was the headman of the Wallowa branch of the Nez Perce,
Tuekakas. He was christened Old Joseph by the local preacher.

Old Joseph's son, born in 1840, was baptised Ephraim (his Indian name
was 'Thunder Rolling In The Valley'), while his brother, born two years
later was called Ollikut (which roughly translates as the less dramatic
'Frog'). But Ephraim would always be known as 'Young Joseph', until his
father's death. The two brothers couldn't be more different. Young Joseph
had the makings of a Civil Chief, was wise and considerate, and was
inclined to 'passive resistance' to the white invaders. He opposed the Nez
Perce factions who wanted war, but he also opposed white supremacy.
Ollikut, by contrast, was groomed for the role of warrior chief, and shared
little of his brother's patience. As a boy, Young Joseph spent much of his
time among the civilised whites at the nearby Lapwai mission, but there
was a certain sense of alienation among the Nez Perce, as half the tribe
became Christians, while the rest remained 'Godless' (insofar as they

didn't recognise a Christian God). Towards the end of the 1840's, more settlers arrived in the area and Old Joseph's band voluntarily moved south into the Wallowa Valley. This group, along with their four nearest neighbours were known thereafter as the 'Lower Nez Perce'. In 1855, the whites decided there should be a treaty, to calculate exactly how much open land there was for white colonisation. The Indians were allotted 10,000 square miles to live within and $200,000. This arrangement was fine until 1860, when gold was discovered on the Nez Perce portion of the area and the gold-hungry prospectors swamped their homeland. When the gold petered out, so did the prospectors, but many stayed behind and settled as farmers. This showed a flagrant disregard for the treaty.

Chief Joseph

To make matters worse, in 1863 revisions were made to the original agreement, unfairly reducing the 10,000 square miles to just 1,000. This wilful act split the Nez Perce down the middle. The Upper Nez Perce under a chief known as Lawyer (so-called for his diplomacy) agreed to this outrage. The Lower branch, with Old Joseph at their head, dissented and stayed in the Wallowa. Old Joseph was severely disenchanted with whites and abandoned Christianity, reverting to the old Indian religion. He became particularly interested in the 'Dreamer' cult, a doctrine preached by a visionary medicine man called Smohalla. This doctrine reinforced Old Joseph's desire to keep hold of his homeland. In 1871, Old Joseph died and his eldest son, Joseph, took over as chief. By this time the whites had decided to take the land (whether there were Indians there or not) and began to settle across the territory. In 1873 Joseph spoke with an agent, who agreed that the 'Upper country' (i.e. the highlands and Wallowa lake) should be given to the Nez Perce, the 'Lower country' (i.e. the valley) to the settlers. Unfortunately, back in Washington, bureaucrats misinterpreted the agreement, reading 'North' for 'Upper' and 'South' for 'Lower', with no thought for topographical details. The new Wallowa Indian Reservation would now occupy the Northern part of the area, which didn't include their beloved Wallowa Lake. Again the government had bungled and the Indians wouldn't budge.

During the subsequent years, tensions between the Indians and whites got worse. The five bands of anti-treaty Nez Perce met at Split Rocks to decide on a course of action. The leaders of each band spoke in turn and voted for peace. But by November 1876 (five months after The Battle Of The Little Big Horn) the army were well and truly fed up with the Nez Perce claim to their birthright to the land. An inconclusive meeting

65

between the Indians and General Howard resulted in General Sherman ordering the anti-treaty bands to the Lapwai Reservation and the suppression of the meddlesome 'Dreamers.' White people would be able to settle in the Wallowa Valley, even if the army had to guard them. General Howard ordered the Indians to be on the reservation in 30 days or face the wrath of the army. Though the deadline was tight, the bands arrived with half a dozen days to spare. Joseph left the camp to round up and slaughter some cattle. But while his peaceful influence was absent, the Dreamers and some hotheads stirred-up trouble. Soon the Indians vented their anger on local whites and 18 were murdered, including women and children. Without Joseph's influence, the leaders of the five bands panicked. One group, under Red Echo (sometimes referred to as Red Owl) went to the reservation. Others, under Chief Looking Glass, headed for Clear Creek, while the bands to whom the guilty Indians belonged, led by White Bird and Too-Hool-Hool-Zote, hid out at White Bird Creek. On his return, Joseph joined this last group. Howard mustered his forces and sent about 100 soldiers under Captain Perry to protect the settlers sheltering in the town of Grangeville. But Perry learned that some of the dissenting Indians were camped at White Bird Creek and he decided to go for glory.

The Trek

On 17 June 1877, Perry's troops approached Joseph's camp on White Bird Creek (located in White Bird Canyon). A party of Indians went out to meet them under a flag of truce, but the troops unsportingly fired on them. The Nez Perce, realising that they were under attack, managed to break up the army attack with their excellent rifle marksmanship. The troops soon broke and fled, but instead of letting them escape, the Indians pursued the depleted force all the way to the settlement of Mount Idaho. Perry lost 34 men, the Nez Perce had no fatalities. In a crucial delay, General Howard was overly cautious and waited for reinforcements while the Indians disappeared. On 22 June, Howard set off and tracked the Indians to the Salmon River. There he spotted a small party of Indians and chased them, finding out too late that they were a diversionary force. The main body of the band had forded the river and gone in another direction. On 1 July Howard resumed his chase and forded the Salmon River and rode into the mountains. The next day, Joseph's party turned back on themselves in a wide arc and recrossed the Salmon 7 miles upstream. Howard, in hot pursuit, followed them across the rough terrain to this second crossing point, but was unable to traverse the river. Howard commandeered a nearby house, took it to pieces and constructed a raft, only to watch as his first attempt at crossing ended in failure. The strong current whisked the raft off down river and into the distance. Outwitted, Howard retraced his steps to exactly the spot where he had begun and crossed the river at White Bird Canyon. By now it was 7 July. On 6 July, Joseph had been joined by Chief Looking Glass's band, which had also run into trouble with the army. After a skirmish in their village, Looking Glass decided that it would be better for the Nez Perce factions to stick together. The news of Joseph's resounding victory over the army at White Bird Creek probably swayed the Chief's decision. Red Echo's group also threw in with Joseph and jumped the reservation. The five bands were together again, and numbered about 700, with only 200 warriors. The troops massing to pursue them dwarfed the Nez Perce 'army', but this particular episode in American history was less about strength in numbers and more about clever tactics. The strange thing was these tactics were those of a pacifist who had never taken to the battlefield in his life.

The Nez Perce rested up near the Clearwater River, convinced that their enemy was far behind, but Howard had unexpectedly caught up with them. On 11 July a cannon blasted out of the hills and the troops attacked. Though he had the element of surprise, Howard was soon on the defensive and formed his troops, some 600 of them, into a circle. By dispersing their men through the hills, timber and gullies, the Indians made it seem as though they were in much greater numbers than they actually were. Consequently 600 men were 'surrounded' by a force a quarter of its size. The fighting continued through the afternoon and into the night. The following day a token force of Nez Perce kept the troops pinned down, while the rest made their escape, crossing the Clearwater on 13 July. Out on the prairie, the Nez Perce had a meeting to decide their next move. One voice would be better than half a dozen, and Chief Looking Glass was elected as leader of the five groups. His suggestion was to head through the Bitterroot Mountains, along the Lolo Trail he had used to hunt buffalo, and so three days later they set off. After the hazardous mountain trek they emerged on 27 July, but their way was blocked by a ramshackle stockade, manned by Captain Rawn (from Fort Missoula), 35 regulars, 200 local volunteers and some Flatheads. The Nez Perce approached under a flag of truce and were pleasantly surprised not to get shot at this time. There they had an inconclusive powwow with the whites. Rawn said they couldn't pass, the Indians didn't want to fight - it was a stalemate. To avoid confrontation, the Nez Perce cunningly bypassed the stockade, by using a narrow path around the hills above the command and descending into the valley beyond. Rawn's barricade was humorously nicknamed 'Fort Fizzle' in honour of this gallant episode.

The Indians pressed on into the Bitterroot Valley and kept friendly with the local settlers. They even went into Stevensville to buy provisions and were careful not to cause trouble. Everything seemed to be going very well and the Nez Perce let their guard down, literally, not even bothering to post sentries or scouts. In the Big Hole Valley on 8 August 1877, several men had ominous visions and a medicine man warned, "Death is on our trail." By first light on 9 August, death wasn't only on their trail, he was watching them, ready to attack. It was Colonel Gibbon, who had driven his men hard from Fort Missoula and had caught up with the hostiles in only five days. He had made double-quick time by carrying his men in wagons and the force of 200 men arrived refreshed and ready to fight. They charged at dawn in a three-pronged attack and ravaged the camp, completely surprising the Indians. Within a short time, the army occupied the camp and the Indians had fled. But Looking Glass and White Bird fought back, rallying their men. They were able to retaliate well enough for the rest of the women and children to escape, though the Nez Perce casualties were much worse this time. In the Battle of Big Hole Joseph's people lost about 80 of their number, many of them women and youngsters. It was their costliest encounter so far and Red Echo, one of the band's leaders, was lying amongst the dead. On 11 August, Howard arrived with reinforcements to bolster Gibbon's decimated force and must have wondered quite what he was up against. Moreover, Howard allowed his Bannock scouts to scalp the dead Nez Perce, which angered Joseph when he learned of the atrocities. Killing women and children was no way to win a war.

On 13 August, General Howard resumed his pursuit and finding the landscape easier going, he started to gain on his quarry. On 18 August, Howard was only a day's march behind the Indians, who were camped out on the Camus Prairie. To slow the General down, Joseph's brother Ollikut raided the army camp and ran-off 200 mules, the loss of which immobilised Howard for three days. By 22 August, the Nez Perce had crossed the Targhee Pass and were heading for Wyoming. They raided farms and wagon trains and, unusually, killed a few white civilians, much to Joseph's chagrin. Looking Glass was worried that the local Crows would be hostile towards them. The Nez Perce chief asked if their old enemies would join them in the fight against a common enemy - the whites. But the Crows only agreed to remain neutral, with no guarantee that the refugees could pass through their territory safely. Instead, the Nez Perce decided to head north, to the Canadian border and sanctuary. Sitting Bull's Sioux band had already fled there earlier that year. The Nez Perce had now travelled about 1000 miles, but it was still a long way to Canada.

Initially the Indians travelled east, through Yellowstone, keeping well wide of Fort Ellis, to the northwest. Then they veered north themselves, and crossed the Yellowstone River. It was on 8 September that the realisation dawned on them that there was a force of soldiers ahead. Colonel Sturgis, with the 7th Cavalry (from Fort Keogh) was waiting for them at Clark's Fork Canyon. The Indians avoided the route, swerving south, and Sturgis followed them. But Joseph's people were again using their cunning rather than force to defeat their enemy and soon struck north, losing the Colonel altogether. An important factor was that they had an excellent half-breed guide, named Poker Joe, who had joined them in the Bitterroot and knew the land like the back of his hand. Sturgis had been led a merry dance and when he finally realised he'd been duped it was too late. He wasted so much time that he eventually rejoined the chase *behind* Howard.

The Sinking Sun

By the 13 September 1877, Sturgis had gained ground and attacked the Nez Perce camp on Canyon Creek. The Indians (in their now trademark style) fought a rearguard action to protect the women, children and elderly as they made their escape, and then blocked their pursuers' route down the canyon with rocks. The Nez Perce pressed on, trying to avoid any more attention from the army, and by the 23 September they had reached the Missouri River. Joseph's keenness for speed was justified. On 17 September, Colonel Miles received a message to mobilise from Fort Keogh. He departed with 600 men and an urge to stop these fugitive Indians making a laughing stock of the army. The Nez Perce column was beginning to suffer for the distance they had travelled. They had been able to trade to get some food, and had attacked an army supply dump on Cow Island, but illness, hunger and battle casualties were starting to slow them down. Their flight ground to a halt on 29 September, at Snake Creek. By now they had travelled 1600 miles. Thinking themselves safe near the Bear Paw Mountains, and presuming their enemies were behind them, they rested. The following morning Colonel Miles attacked. Surprised, Joseph must have felt that his people couldn't withstand another expensive attack. Miles' first charge was astonishingly repulsed by the Nez Perce marksmen, and Miles decided to throw his troops into a ring around the camp and lay siege. The Indians dug in and waited.

Afternoon brought a fresh attack, but again the Indians repulsed it. By evening the true cost of the fight emerged - amongst the dead were their guide Poker Joe, Chief Too-Hool-Hool-Zote and Joseph's brother Ollikut. Perhaps for the first time, Joseph felt like the end of their journey was close at hand. In the night it snowed and a blast of artillery was the Nez Perce wake-up call on 1 October. But the siege was an impasse and at noon Miles gave the Indians the chance to parley. Joseph went to negotiate - he wanted to return to Idaho, but Miles wanted total surrender. Neither would budge and with no conclusion in sight Miles chivalrously took the chief hostage, though he was only held overnight. The Bear Paws deadlock was broken on the evening of 4 October when General Howard arrived with reinforcements. On 5 October, Joseph was again offered a surrender and this time he gave it more thought. His people were freezing to death and starving, and he resolved to capitulate for their sakes. But there was one last tragedy, before a surrender could be signed. A rider approached the camp that afternoon and Looking Glass was convinced he was friendly. Going to greet the rider the chief was shot by what turned out to be one of Miles' Indian scouts. He died where he fell, the last military fatality of the Nez Perce trek. That meant that of the chiefs who had left the Wallowa in June, only Joseph and White Bird were still alive. So on 5 October 1877, Joseph went out to meet Miles and Howard. Face to face, Joseph proffered his rifle to Howard, who passed and allowed Miles to accept Joseph's surrender - after all, it was he who had saved face and finally cornered the hostiles. After their surrender, the Nez Perce were treated just as unfairly as every other Indian tribe under the white government. Joseph presumed that they would be returned to Idaho, but they were marched first to Fort Keogh and then on to Fort Lincoln, North Dakota. Not all the Nez Perce made the journey. White Bird and about 28 followers managed to escape to Canada, while the truce was being finalised. By late November, the Nez Perce were taken to Kansas and told to live in a malaria-infested swamp near Fort Leavenworth. The disease eventually forced the Bureau of Indian Affairs to move them yet again, to the sultry (and unsuitable) climate of the Quapaw Indian Reservation and finally, in 1889, to the Lapwai Reservation in Idaho. But Joseph wasn't allowed to go to Idaho and was sent with 150 others to the Colville Reservation in Washington State. Through all these trials, Joseph remained stoic and uncomprehending of the white man's inability to tell the truth. But he was deeply saddened, lamenting, "The Great Spirit seemed to be looking the other way, and did not see what was being done to my people." He appealed for years to return to the lush Wallowa, but his pleas fell on deaf ears. He even went to Washington to talk to President McKinley, to no avail. Joseph travelled to the Wallowa only once after his surrender, in 1899, and visited his father's grave. He died five years later. Rather poetically, the cause of death given by the camp doctor was a broken heart.

But Joseph will be remembered, more than anything, for his statesmanship and his way with words - words that could calm hot-tempered braves and negotiate with generals. His speech of surrender to Miles and Howard has passed into American history as one of the saddest moments of the Indian Wars. A moment when a man not only knows when he is beaten, but also truly comprehends what he has lost in the fight for what he believes in. His words are worth repeating here:

"I am tired of fighting. Our chiefs are killed. Looking Glass is dead. Too-Hool-Hool-Zote is dead. The old men are all killed. It is the young men who say yes or no. He who has led the young men (Joseph's brother Ollikut) is dead. It is cold and we have no blankets. The little children are freezing to death. I want time to look for my children, and see how many of them I can find. Maybe I shall find them among the dead. Hear me, my chiefs. I am tired, my heart is sick and sad. From where the sun now stands, I will fight no more forever."

Requiem Apache

'If you owned Hell and Arizona, live in Hell and rent out
Arizona.'

To the south of the Great Plains were the flaming deserts of Arizona,
New Mexico and Texas, down to the Mexican border. This land was no
good for farming. It was an arid, sandblasted landscape filled with rattle-
snakes, jackrabbits and Indians. As a reflection of the stark landscape of
deserts and mountains, there lived the toughest of the native warrior tribes.
The Comanche, Kiowa, Navajo, Pueblo and most famous of all, the
Apache. The Apache were a warrior race, stocky and resilient, who lived
off the land. Game was sparse, water scarce, but somehow the Indians survived in the inhospitable climate, living among the rocks, down canyons, in
caves and in tangled thickets of brush. They were one tribe who were really
at one with the land.

The Apache Wars

The Apache were subdivided into several groups, amongst which were
the Mimbreno, Chiricahua, Mascalero, Jacarilla, Kiowa-Apache and Western Apache. They roamed through West Texas, Arizona, New Mexico and
both sides of the Mexican border, clashing with the local Americans and
Mexicans. The Mexicans were happy to sustain an uneasy peace with the
Indians, but it was always on a knife-edge. In the 1700's, the Hispanics had
tried to rid the area of Apache, with inter-tribal warfare, and by encourag-
ing a reliance on rations and alcohol. If these three things could have been
controlled then the Spanish would have succeeded. Many Apache settled
down and the system was quite successful until the Apache sensed that the
Spanish power was weakening in the area, with the arrival of more Americans. In the 1820's the Mimbreno, under Juan Jose Compa, had allowed the
Spanish to mine copper at Pinos Altos, near Santa Rita del Cobre, but half
the tribe under Cuchillo Negro ('Black Knife') disagreed, forming their
own splinter group at Warm Springs.

In 1831, the Apaches living near the copper mine struck a treaty with the
Spanish, but the weaknesses in the Spanish regime were becoming apparent. When the promised rations for the Apache didn't materialise, they
went on the warpath - raiding and stealing horses. This encouraged the Hispanics to renew their attempts to rid the area of Apache. Instead of an
attempt at reconciliation, the Mexican Junta offered bounties for the scalps
of Apache warriors, offering a 100-peso reward for every one brought in.

Things escalated when this offer was extended to women and children, which would net the scalphunters 50 pesos and 25 pesos respectively. Sometimes the officials wanted the ears of the victims included, so that the greedy hunters couldn't split the scalps and get twice their worth. The Indians had no real hatred of the whites and Mexicans until this law was introduced. The bounties attracted scalphunters from miles around, the most notorious of whom were James Kirker (known as 'The King of New Mexico') and James Johnson, a trader from Kentucky. Johnson in particular, was responsible for one of the most brutal episodes of the period. He recruited a gang of American cutthroats and rode to the Santa Rita mines with the Mexican government's blessing. To up the ante, the mine owners even offered more money on top of the bounties. In April 1837, all the local Apache (the 'Copper Mine People') were invited to a great feast. Not just the warriors, but their wives and children too. It was seen as a gesture of goodwill by the mine owners. The Indians were fed and liberally plied with liquor, but unbeknownst to them the feast was a set-up. Hidden in the brush was a cannon. As the Indians celebrated, Johnson fired the cannon point-blank into the revellers. Accounts of the carnage vary significantly, recording casualties varying from 20 to 400. The chief, Juan Jose, was killed but another leader present, Mangas Coloradas, escaped with his life. United in their hatred of the whites, the scattered Apache factions (including the Copper Mine and Warm Springs groups) bonded, with Coloradas their new head man.

Mangas Coloradas

Mangas Coloradas was perhaps the cleverest and most strategically aware of the Apache chiefs. He earned his name when he appropriated a fur hunter's red flannel shirt in battle, the garment literally translating as 'Red Sleeves.' Though he was cruel, he was also a reasonable man. He was a Mimbreno Apache and stood an impressive six feet seven inches tall. Realising that there would be no way for the Americans, Mexicans and Apache to live together he mobilised his force and began attacking any strangers, be they trappers, homesteaders or townspeople. Thus Mangas Coloradas held Santa Rita in the grip of terror. No supplies could get through. In a bizarre decision, the mayor decided that there were too few soldiers to defend the town. If he sent them out as a recce party the population would have to go with them. The entire town, some 400 men, women and children, packed up their belongings and set off south into the desert. What happened next is not known. The six survivors who eventually made their way to the settlement at Janos were too traumatised to give an account of their ordeal.

In his war, Coloradas used several neighbouring chiefs as his 'generals', including Victorio and Cuchillo Negro, while others became his allies through marriage (as in the case of Cochise, who married Mangas Coloradas' daughter). They mercilessly raided Mexican settlements like Sonora and Durango, killing and looting. In 1846 the Americans and Mexicans went to war against each other. During this conflict, many of the Pueblo Indians sided with the Mexicans, to try and get rid of the Americans. The bloody uprising cost many lives but achieved little and the Indian ringleaders were shot or hung. The Mexicans hadn't backed their allies up and soon afterwards the Americans, having won the war, controlled most of the area. By 1848, gold had been discovered in California and the Gold Rush was on. Like the Black Hills Gold Rush years later, the area was swamped with wagons and prospectors heading West, sitting ducks for the raiding Apache who killed and tortured the men, and rode away with the women and children to an uncertain fate. A group of Americans (a surveying party and their army escort) temporarily reoccupied Santa Rita, but the pervading atmosphere of tension and violence encouraged them to move on. Mangas Coloradas was itching for trouble and he soon found it. Three years after the Californian gold strike, the same discovery was made at Pinos Alto which brought even more intruders to the area. Coloradas went into the camp alone to tell the miners that he could show them a rich vein of the yellow metal. It is not known whether he was being entirely honest, but the miners sensed a trap and decided to have a little fun. They tied him up and savagely whipped him, but they made one crucial mistake - they left him alive. Mangas Coloradas' thirst for vengeance would result in much bloodletting.

Cochise

Coloradas enlisted the help of Cochise, chief of the Chiricahua Apache. Cochise wasn't that hateful of the whites until the 'Bascom Incident' of 1861, when he and his men were wrongly accused of stealing a young boy from a ranch. The boy had actually been taken by Pinal Apaches, though some sources claim that he accidentally wandered off from the ranch, or that he ran away from his alcoholic stepfather. Whatever, the officer put in charge of the search, Lieutenant Bascom, decided that Cochise was responsible. He went to the stage station in Apache Pass, to capture the chief. In the ensuing fight, Cochise took six prisoners and the troops took five warriors. A trade was proposed, but never transpired. The troops got reinforcements and the Indians withdrew, though not before executing all their prisoners. The army replied by hanging their captives and Cochise never trusted the whites again.

Cochise joined Mangas Coloradas at a crucial period in American history. The Civil War had just begun and many of the troops on the frontier were withdrawn to fight in the east. This left the remaining whites poorly protected and easy pickings for the war parties. But in 1862 the War between the States spilled West, and Union and Confederate forces appeared in the area, vying for important lines of communication around Valverde and Santa Fe. Inevitably the Indians got involved, attacking supply trains, killing stragglers and running-off horses. The Confederates occupied the recently deserted stockades and fought with the Indians over the mines in Pinos Alto. In 1862, the Apaches, under Mangas Coloradas and Cochise, learned of a large Union force heading eastwards to the main theatre of war. The Unionists didn't want to fight the Indians. They were on their way somewhere else to fight a completely different enemy. To the Apache, a white was a white and they prepared a huge ambush in Apache Pass. The largest force of warriors in the Apache Wars was assembled for the attack, but it would be the last action of its type - Cochise and Coloradas learned much from this engagement.

The Union force under Captain Roberts knew nothing of frontier warfare and walked straight into the trap. The Indians forced the troops to withdraw and then pinned them down. The troops needed water from the springs in Apache Pass and decided to force their way through. Using their artillery to excellent advantage, they broke through to the water supply. With reinforcements on the way, the troops could consolidate their position, but the battle had cost the Indians one important casualty. In a skirmish nearby with a group of soldiers from Roberts' column, Mangas Coloradas was shot and wounded. His men took him to the doctor in the Mexican settlement of Janos (120 miles away) and told him that if Coloradas died the town would cease to exist. With such an ultimatum, it was only natural for Coloradas to make a full recovery.

The Unionists defeated the Confederates decisively in 1862 at the Battle of Glorietta Pass. With the rebels abandoning the area, the army could concentrate on clearing the area of Apaches and Navajos. Fort Bowie was constructed in Apache Pass to keep the route open and the water accessible. But by 1863, Coloradas (now aged about 70) had tired of fighting and went to Pinos Alto to make peace with the troops guarding the gold mine. The soldiers captured him and the officer in command made it obvious that he didn't want the notorious chief to last the night. He was tortured with red-hot bayonets and when he protested, was summarily shot dead at point-blank range. The official line was that Coloradas had been killed trying to escape. Cochise's war on the whites changed dramatically after the Battle of Apache Pass and the death of Mangas Coloradas. He never attacked large groups of troops in the open and adopted guerrilla-style hit-and-run tactics to make the most of his resources. The element of surprise was his greatest weapon. Cochise's treatment of white captives got considerably worse too, as his men perfected the art of torture which kept their victims alive for hours and guaranteed them a lingering death. He was joined in his war by the chiefs Victorio and Nana and the famed warrior Geronimo. But no matter how many whites they killed, more came in their place. It seemed as though the prospectors, settlers and soldiers were oblivious to the incredible dangers that lurked in the thickets, canyons and mountains. When someone coined the phrase, "If you owned Hell and Arizona, live in Hell and rent out Arizona", they were only partly thinking about the climate.

Geronimo

His original name was Goyahkla, or 'One Who Yawns', but the mention of Geronimo's name to anyone in the American Southwest rarely produced a bored reaction, but rather hysteria. Contrary to popular belief, he was never an Apache chief, but a brave maverick Indian who had the guts to lead war parties when the older chiefs (like Nana) lost the nerve to fight. He also believed he was bullet-proof. In the summer of 1858 Geronimo's band had camped near the town of Janos to trade with the Mexicans. While the warriors were away bartering, Mexican troops attacked the camp and slaughtered the women and children with bayonets. Among the dead were Geronimo's wife (Alope), his mother and three children. Returning, Geronimo burned his home and all his family's possessions. He, more than any other Apache, had ample reason to loathe the invaders. "None had lost as I had", he said, "For I had lost all." In retribution for the death of his entire family, Geronimo, with Mangas Coloradas' blessing, attacked and massacred the Mexican town of Arispe. Because he had lost his family to the Mexicans, Geronimo was allowed to direct the revenge. He drew the Mexican garrison out and a pitched battle ensued. It was in this battle that 'One Who Yawns' got the name Geronimo. His attacks on the Mexicans were so ferocious and fanatical that the troops cried for divine intervention from St Jerome (Geronimo in Spanish). The Apache also took up the cry and a legend was born. Strangely, some sources reverse the order of these two significant events, saying that the Mexican massacre of Apaches at Janos was in response to the attack on Arispe, while others say that the battle didn't take place at Arispe at all, but 20 miles away at Stinking Wells.

Geronimo tended to raid into Mexico, rather than attacking Yankee outposts, though he'd been present at the Bascom Incident and the Battle of Apache Pass. With the death of Mangas Coloradas, Geronimo and Cochise vowed to fight on in his memory. The army decided to take no chances and issued the order - kill every Indian capable of bearing arms, and capture the women and children. Mangas Coloradas' successor among the Mimbreno was Victorio, who had learned well from his mentor. The wars continued until 1869, when the Americans realised this 'No Mercy' policy wasn't working. The Apache were difficult to find and the war would never be conclusive. Eventually Victorio settled on a reservation and the following year a peace council almost convinced the other chiefs to come in, though Cochise and Geronimo didn't oblige. In 1871, General Crook became commander of the Department Of Arizona. A cunning Indian fighter, the Apache called him 'Chief Grey Wolf'. He employed Apache scouts, which proved much more effective against his invisible, guerrilla foe. In 1872, one-armed Civil War veteran General Howard finally convinced Cochise to surrender. Tired of fighting, and promised land in Apache Pass near Fort Bowie, Cochise complied. But after two years of being shunted from one reservation to another, Cochise became very ill and subsequently died. For two years there was peace, though the raiding continued, with the Indians proudly bringing their booty back to the reservation. In 1875, with Crook removed to fight the Sioux, the government adopted a 'Concentration Policy' to get all the Indians together in one place. Petty marauding by the Indians and complaints from the Mexicans finally gave the authorities the excuse to put their plan into action. The place the Apache ended up was the San Carlos Reservation, christened, without irony, 'Hell's Forty Acres' which was riddled with disease, corruption, inter-tribal disputes and poor food supplies. Geronimo had his doubts about reservation life and in 1876 he escaped into Mexico. It was obvious that the authorities were going to have their hands full.

Last Of The Renegades

Throughout the winter of 1876-77, Geronimo and his band avoided the army, but the tough weather took its toll on his followers. In March 1877, Geronimo rode out of Mexico with a herd of stolen horses. He crossed the border to trade the steeds, but a local Indian Agent, John Clum, heard of Geronimo's whereabouts and captured him. Incarcerated in San Carlos, Geronimo wasn't interested in farming and other peaceful activities, and was itching to resume his raids. The poor living conditions, outbreaks of disease (like smallpox and malaria) and crooked traders exploiting the Indians made Geronimo's mind drift to thoughts of the wild mountains of the Sierra Madre. When troops were brought in to guard the Indians, in place of the Indian Police, Victorio and his band immediately left the reservation to begin raiding, forcing the American and Mexican armies to mount a joint offensive against his band. Victorio, a clever tactician in the manner of Mangas Coloradas, proved a formidable foe. However, his vow to 'make war forever' on the US proved highly inaccurate. He was ambushed and killed by the Mexican General Terrazas in the mountains in 1880, but the elderly chief Nana took over and continued Victorio's campaign.

In early 1881, a fanatical religion akin to the Sioux 'Ghost Dance' and the Nez Perce 'Dreamer' cult, became popular with the desert reservation Indians. They believed that their dead chiefs and warriors would be resurrected in a battle with the whites. In September, the army were called in to stamp out this movement and rumour spread that Geronimo would be hanged. Understandably jumpy, Geronimo and 70 men made for the Sierra Madre mountains. In April 1882 Geronimo returned to San Carlos, but not as a prisoner. He was there to convince the other Apaches under Loco to come to Mexico. As they made a dash for the border, the army caught up with them. The warriors tried to hold the troops off, while the women and children escaped. Unfortunately, this helpless vanguard ran headlong into a Mexican Infantry Regiment. Most of the women and children were killed, but many of the warriors escaped, including Geronimo himself. He joined Nana's band, to form a group of about 80 warriors. Over the next two years, Geronimo's men raided through Mexico, and also into the States. Attacks on farms and ranches meant that the government recalled bewhiskered, mule-riding General Crook to tackle the Apache once more. After finding that the conditions were pitiful on the reservation, Crook realised why Geronimo was so keen to live in the mountains. He tried to improve the Apaches' living conditions and then set about getting Geronimo back in the camp. It was obvious Geronimo was raiding into the States again. His warriors struck a mining camp in Arizona and a few days later killed a New Mexican judge. Crook reacted swiftly and set off in pursuit, with his cavalry troops swelled by 193 Apache scouts - a major innovation as now Crook knew the land as well as his quarry. "Only an Apache can catch an Apache", ran a proverb, though Crook was the first soldier to put this into practice.

In May 1883, his scouts found and attacked a group of Geronimo's party. Though there were few casualties, the Apache were amazed at how they had been surprised in what they thought was the impenetrable Sierra

Madre. Tired of running, or perhaps content to rest for a while, Geronimo agreed to meet Crook and surrender. The raiders arrived at San Carlos in March the following year and lived peaceably for a time. But the 'peace', as it was, couldn't last forever. One night Geronimo got drunk with several other chiefs on the lethal brew Tizwin (corn liquor). The consumption of alcohol by reservation Indians was not permitted and Geronimo apprehensively waited to see how he would be punished. Worried of reprisals, he again fled into Mexico with about 130 followers. Crook was livid and, riding his faithful mule 'Apache', he set off in pursuit. This time he was taking no chances however and his force comprised of 3000 men (including 200 friendly Indian scouts). Through the winter of 1885-86, Crook doggedly hunted Geronimo through the Sierra Madre, realising that he was getting closer all the time to his prey. In March 1886, Geronimo met Crook to discuss the terms of surrender (March seemed to be Geronimo's favourite month to give himself up), but before the general could get him across the border, Geronimo broke his word and fled with 20 warriors and 18 camp followers.

Crook was severely criticised for his plodding pursuit and failure to catch Geronimo. What did he expect, trying to catch a band of swift, experienced guerrilla fighters on a mule. On April Fools' Day 1886 he requested a transfer and his superiors obliged, replacing him with General Miles, who had been the officer who stopped Chief Joseph's Nez Perce from reaching the Canadian border (and safety) nine years before. His orders left nothing to the imagination - 'capture or destroy.' Miles' first action was to shift all the Apaches (including Crook's friendly scouts) to Florida. Then in 1886, he began his offensive with 5000 troops, a different bunch of scouts and another frontier innovation, the heliograph, a Morse signalling system using mirrors. This way, news could be flashed long distances in double-quick time. Miles then split his force into small groups, so whenever there was a sign of trouble, the heliograph could alert troops in the locality and they would be straight on the raiders' trail. Even with all this technology, Geronimo still made Miles feel like he was chasing ghosts. The wily Apache surfaced and vanished - attacking a ranch in Arizona, then the town of Nogales - with no deaths in his party. Miles had a rethink and asked Geronimo to negotiate.

In August 1886, Geronimo met with Miles' envoy, Lieutenant Gatewood, and learned that his family, indeed his whole people, had been shipped off to Florida. Geronimo was destroyed by the news and agreed to parley with Miles. He had lost the will to fight and wanted to see his family. Previously, he had hedged his bets and surrendered when it suited him. Now it would be his final submission. On his arrival at Fort Pickens (on

Santa Rosa Island, off Florida) he was put in prison for two years without seeing his family. Even worse, the warriors' wives and children were moved to Fort Marion, 300 miles away. In all, Geronimo spent 23 years in captivity, first in Florida, later in Southern Oklahoma, but he never returned to his beloved Arizona. He died in 1909 of pneumonia, aged approximately 80. He was the last of the Indian rebels to surrender. As a young man he had traded horses, rode free and struck terror into the hearts of every person in the dusty Southwest. As an old man he peddled autographs and home-made bows and arrows, and was exhibited before his enemies as a freak show, a 'Real Live Injun' - a truly sad reflection of the taming of the West.

Savage Messiah

'As the white man comes in, the Indian goes out'

The Battle of the Little Big Horn was the biggest defeat inflicted on the US Army during the Indian Wars, but the repercussions for the Indians were immense. When Sitting Bull and Crazy Horse led their people out of the Big Horn Valley on the evening of 26 June 1876, little did they know what the next few years would hold in store. Custer's Last Stand was big news, and both the government and the army were under fire to subdue the hostiles. The government reiterated that any Indians not confined to reservations were dangerous and set about bringing the remaining renegades into custody. In his prophecy before the Battle of the Little Big Horn, Sitting Bull had been told that the soldiers falling into his camp were gifts from the gods, but his warriors must not loot the soldiers. The Indians had ignored this aspect of the sacred deal. Sitting Bull knew the gods would want revenge - and so would the army.

Scalps For Custer

After the Little Big Horn fight, the huge Indian camp split. The two main groups were led by Crazy Horse and Sitting Bull, while many others went back to reservations. Even a chief of Sitting Bull's stature couldn't keep the fractious plains tribes together indefinitely. Meanwhile, though General Crook had suffered a severe setback at the Battle of the Rosebud (and on 10 July was one of the last people in the entire country to find out about the Custer massacre), he was ready to remobilize by mid-July. His command was beefed-up with some welcome reinforcements, including the 5th Cavalry under Colonel Merritt. Merritt had been delayed from joining Crook. En route he had heard a report that 800 Cheyenne had escaped from the Red Cloud Agency and were heading to join up with the renegades. Merritt cut the Indians off at Warbonnet Creek on 17 July 1876 and herded them back to the reservation. It was during this manoeuvre that the celebrated duel between Buffalo Bill Cody and Cheyenne chief Yellow Hair took place, an encounter that gained mythical status in the West, being compared to the duel between Achilles and Hector from 'The Iliad' (Cody won). This detour by the 5th Cavalry delayed Crook's campaign departure, but Merritt was commended for his actions - the soldiers could do without an extra 800 Cheyenne opponents. The army's main offensive eventually got underway in August 1876. During this campaign, which ran from 1876 to mid-1877, many of the army's most formidable and well-known Indian fighters were employed - familiar names such as Crook, Terry, Miles and Mackenzie were all involved in this concentrated effort to disperse and destroy the Indian bands. The initial thrust was led by Crook and Terry. Crook had about 2000 men, including his Shoshonis under Washakie. Terry also had about 2000 men, including Miles' slow moving infantry column. But the landscape was formidable, the pace gruelling and by the beginning of September, Terry's force had fallen by the wayside. Though it was seen as defeatist at the time, Terry's decision seemed to be a phenomenal case of foresight, especially when one learns of what happened to Crook.

Crook persevered. His men wished he hadn't, but that was the general's way. In late August the rain fell and turned the trails into quagmires. The horses floundered and Crook's column got bogged down. To make matters worse, one of Crook's clever plans backfired. He had his soldiers ditch their supply wagons before they set out on the march. The column was travelling light, supposedly for speed. But their enemy didn't materialise and as the offensive dragged on, the troops' scant supplies ran out. Gradually, the men began to starve. The first thing to run out was the coffee. Everything else went the same way. The soldiers went swiftly from hunger to famine. The unrelenting rain completely destroyed their resolve and their sanity. Finally, in a desperate situation, they started to eat their own horses, though one trooper later commented that he'd rather have eaten his own brother. By 7 September Crook took action and sent Captain Mills (Crook's saviour at the Battle of the Rosebud), to go and get some supplies from the mining town of Deadwood. Two days later Mills inadvertently found the Sioux camp of Iron Plume, near Slim Buttes. The inhabitants were Miniconjou and Oglala, both of whom had been present at the Little Big Horn. Mills, though exhausted, attacked at dawn and kept attacking until Crook caught up later that day. The starving force destroyed the village, captured food and repulsed a strike by Crazy Horse. During the attack the soldiers recovered much cavalry property, including a 7th Cavalry flag carried at the Little Big Horn, a pair of gauntlets bearing Colonel Keogh's name, cavalry horses, items of clothing and weapons - proof positive that these hostiles had been involved in butchering Custer. Mills' assault was particularly vicious (killing many women and children), but the cavalry wanted revenge for their dead comrades. The troops were calling themselves 'Custer's Avengers' and every scalp taken was 'a scalp for Custer.' But Slim Buttes was the end of Crook's campaign - his force was so debilitated that any further combat would have finished it off. With unusual understatement a journalist with Crook's column wrote, 'The general impression in this command is that we have not so much to boast of in the way of killing Indians.' The debacle was christened variously 'The Horse Meat March', 'The Mud March' and 'The Starvation March' (with the survivors described as scarecrows), and was almost the Donner Party misadventure on a grand scale. Crook started out with a cavalry troop and ended up with infantry.

Miles and Mackenzie took up the baton, safe in the knowledge that any kind of result would be better than Crook's. On 25 November Mackenzie attacked Dull Knife's Cheyenne village and razed it. Miles, unperturbed by the severe winter weather kept his infantry after the Sioux in a series of running battles. Meanwhile a rehabilitated Crook periodically joined the campaign, then stalled in the snow and gave up the chase. Crook was damn near unbeatable in the desert, but ineffective in inclement weather. He never understood the need to harass the Indians in their winter camps or when to press home an advantage (when the rare opportunity arose that he had one). Miles continued his campaign into the New Year. His 350-man force was attacked by Crazy Horse's forces (numbering about 500 warriors) on 7 January at Wolf Mountain. Miles made full use of his artillery (which he had disguised as supply wagons) in the snowbound terrain and the Indians eventually broke and fled the field, under cover of a blizzard. The Battle of Wolf Mountain changed Crazy Horse's opinion of the army. He realised that the troops were getting more tenacious. Moreover, support for the peace movement was growing in his village. Soon afterward the Indians melted away into smaller groups. Sitting Bull escaped to Canada in late January 1877. He requested that the Sioux be recognised as British and given shelter in Canada (the Sioux had fought with the British during the American Revolution). The Canadians tolerated the Sioux, but vetoed this plea for token citizenship. Back in the States, the army sensed that cracks were beginning to show in the tribes. The white authorities convinced the chief of the reservation Sioux, Spotted Tail, to visit Crazy Horse's camp and proffer peace. Spotted Tail was a welcome sight for many of the starving, shivering Sioux and he convinced many Indians to give up. By May 1877, with supplies and morale low, even Crazy Horse submitted. He rode into the Red Cloud Agency on 6 May and turned himself in to the authorities. Apart from Sitting Bull, languishing in Canada, there was only one Sioux holdout - a chief named Lame Deer. General Miles found his camp on the Rosebud on 7 May and burned it. Lame Deer agreed to surrender, but the negotiations degenerated into a shoot-out. A bullet narrowly missed Miles, while Lame Deer was shot and killed.

Crazy Horse Is Broken

Once on a reservation, many of the other Indians were jealous of Crazy Horse. He held too much sway with the hothead elements dreaming of another war. Plots began to surface to get rid of him. Some of the Indians, as jealous of his celebrity as much as his power, offered a bounty of $100 (plus a horse) to kill him. With no takers, they deliberately stirred up trouble between the whites and Crazy Horse. The army issued an order that Crazy Horse should be arrested when the rumourmongers claimed that Crazy Horse was ready to go back on the warpath. Crazy Horse was arrested at Fort Robinson on 6 September 1877, but when he saw that he was going to be cooped-up in a cell and chained, he panicked. Crazy Horse had played right into his enemies' hands. A struggle was what the army and many reservation Indians wanted. His captors thought that he was trying to escape and, restraining him, bayoneted him to death. Crazy Horse died during the night in his father's arms. Betrayed by his one-time allies and friends, it was a disgraceful death for such a brave warrior.

By 1878 most of the Plains Indians had been pacified. Only Sitting Bull's Sioux band was at large and they weren't even in their own country. But as the expatriate Sioux's food supplies ran low, they returned across the border to hunt. General Miles went to apprehend Sitting Bull, but the wily Indian knew the power of the border and skedaddled back to Canada. Miles, showing remarkable restraint, let him go. Over the years of his exile, Sitting Bull had become dependent on traders for their supplies, which were bought on credit. The traders, fully aware that the Indians couldn't pay their debts, foreclosed and Sitting Bull was forced to return to the States. Eventually the army got what they wanted and Sitting Bull at last gave up, at Fort Buford on 19 July 1881. The army promised him an amnesty, but instead kept him in prison at Fort Randall for 2 years on the preposterous pretext of Custer's murder. Then in 1883 he was finally sent to the reservation at Standing Rock. Fed up with reservation life, he joined Buffalo Bill's travelling 'Wild West Show' in 1885, effectively as an exhibit. His appearances were extremely popular, but there was also sometimes the whiff of exploitation. During one performance, Sitting Bull gave an oration in his native language. A young Sioux in the audience realised the irony of the performance. Sitting Bull was telling the non-Sioux speaking audience that he was pleased the war was over and extolling the benefits of good education for the young. Then a white intermediary stood up and gave the audience the 'translation', a sensationalistic account of the Battle of the Little Big Horn. Sitting Bull also appeared in quaint dramatisations of Sioux life - as a sort of living museum piece. That said, Sitting

Bull loved the celebrity such appearances brought him, which by contrast made his reservation life very dull indeed. In 1888, the government decided they wanted to buy 11,000,000 acres of open Sioux territory for the insulting sum of 50 cents an acre. Sitting Bull and others opposed it, but the government 'purchased' it all the same.

Ghost Dance

Of the many cults that swept through the Indian tribes over the years, the Ghost Dance was the most powerful. Perhaps it seemed so powerful because the Indians were stuck on reservations and had run out of hope. When visionaries came before, the Indians had a clear choice between following the doctrine or ignoring it. Now they had no option but to trust in magic. Mysticism was going to be the only way they could escape from their servile drudgery. A combination of exploitation, measles and drought had destroyed the Indians' resolve, their health and their crops. On New Year's Day 1889 a Paiute Indian named Wovoka had a vision from the gods. The vision told him that the Indians must perform a sacred mass ritual known as the Ghost Dance. If the Indians did this, it would bring about an utopian existence, where the buffalo roamed the plains and the ghosts of the Indians' dead ancestors would return. Furthermore, the whites would mysteriously vanish from the Indians' homeland without the Indians lifting a finger. The Indians must not be aggressive to their enemies - the gods would take care of the whites. It was strange that the authorities, not really understanding what the Ghost Dance was about, found Wovoka's 'peaceful' teachings to be a threat and sought to control, and if necessary stamp out, the cult.

Within months the Ghost Dance spread like wildfire. The Indians were eager to be reacquainted with their ancestors, though the way many eventually achieved this wasn't in Wovoka's original plan. By 1890 the cult had reached the Sioux, via the mystic Kicking Bear. Sitting Bull invited Kicking Bear to demonstrate the salvation dance to his tribe. For the shuffling dance the participants wore decorated Ghost Shirts, which they believed to be bullet-proof. The ceremonies were on a huge scale and went on for hours and sometimes days. The whites saw the potential for revolt, with the participants going into a mystical trance. Any man who believes he's bullet proof and has a grudge against you is going to be tricky to handle, pacifist or not. The authorities, already nervous about Wovoka's influence, decided to take action when they heard that Sitting Bull was getting involved with these fanatics. Major McLaughlin, an Indian Agent, hated Sitting Bull and had been searching for an excuse to get rid of the chief. The Ghost Dance permeating the Hunkpapas provided it. On 12 December McLaughlin ordered the arrest of Sitting Bull. As a further insult, the agent sent the Indian Police (turncoat Indians who policed their own people) to bring the chief into custody. Perhaps McLaughlin knew Sitting Bull wouldn't stand for that. On dawn of 15 December 1890, 40 Indian Police (obviously expecting trouble) went to Sitting Bull's cabin and arrested him. Sitting Bull wouldn't budge and in the confusion, Sitting Bull's men were alerted. In the ensuing fracas, Sitting Bull took two bullets in the back. But there were further casualties - Sitting Bull's son Crow Foot, Jumping Bull (Sitting Bull's adopted brother) and Jumping Bull's son Chase Them Wounded were all killed by the police, along with about ten others. The authorities seemed to be trying to discontinue the Sitting Bull dynasty. The great chief's body was beaten and disfigured after his death and the remains were interred at Fort Yates on 17 December 1890. The army private who made the box said later that he was constantly interrupted by soldiers who wanted to drive a nail into the chief's coffin.

Battle Of Wounded Knee

Some of Sitting Bull's band surrendered, but about 40 went on the run and joined Chief Big Foot's Miniconjou camp. Big Foot was also keen on the Ghost Dance and was horrified to hear of Sitting Bull's death. The Miniconjou chief was a strong advocate of Wovoka's teachings and the authorities were wary of him. Big Foot's influence within his tribe was great and he was perceived as one of the last holdouts. Some sources say that the army actually issued an order to arrest Big Foot, while others say that Big Foot merely suspected that he would be targeted. Either way, Big Foot and his 300 followers bolted into the snow-covered badlands on the day before Christmas Eve 1890. The army reacted quickly and despite the appalling conditions they were soon in hot pursuit, with General Miles at their head. By the time the troops caught up with the fugitives on 28 December, Big Foot was laid-up with pneumonia. The Indians didn't resist and were quietly escorted to Wounded Knee Creek. There they would be disarmed and returned to the reservation, as per the army's orders. The officer in charge of this delicate operation was Colonel Forsyth, who was now in charge of the resurrected version of Custer's old regiment, the 7th Cavalry. Unconfirmed reports imply that Forsyth's orders stipulated that he get Big Foot and his followers out of the area as quickly as possible - rushing them to a railway depot and off to Omaha for a spell behind bars. But he never got the chance. To safeguard against escape, the army had positioned four cannons around the Indian camp, and by the morning of 29 December there were about 500 soldiers on site.

The Indians were lined up and disarmed, then their tepees were searched for further weapons. In the middle of this indignity a medicine man named Yellow Bird decided to start Ghost Dancing. The tension between the two groups was palpable, when suddenly a rifle went off. One of the Indians didn't feel like handing over his prized Winchester and it went off accidentally. The soldiers reacted quickly and without thinking. They fired a volley straight at the Indians, who armed themselves and engaged the troops in hand-to-hand combat. As the melee developed the army's cannons were brought to bear on the camp and loosed a savage barrage. Then as suddenly as it had begun the battle was over, but the resulting scene was of utter devastation. The Indians' lodges burned, the snow was stained with blood and nearly half of Big Foot's band had been annihilated. There was later confirmation that at least 150 Sioux had perished - men, women and children alike. The soldiers withdrew from the battlefield, taking the wounded Indians in wagons, but they could do nothing with the dead, as a blizzard blew in making conditions impossible. The snowstorm covered all signs of the atrocity and obliterated the scene under a peaceful white blanket.

On New Year's Day 1891, the army burial parties returned to Wounded Knee Creek to prise the frozen, contorted corpses from the snow and heap them into pits. Army photographers captured the morbid moment for posterity in a series of sepia prints. Among the dead was Big Foot. A couple of the photographs depict his frozen death pose, lying on his back on the Wounded Knee battlefield, his hands contorted as though he's playing an imaginary guitar. It is a melancholy picture of an old man in death that is often used to illustrate the definitive end of the Indians. But any one of hundreds of photographs, lithographs, sketches and paintings could easily be substituted for the picture of Big Foot. The heaps of buffalo hides, the booming towns, the railroad, the disease epidemics and the miles of wagon trains were what destroyed the Indians - not the army. In the 1490's, when America was first colonised by Europeans, there were 10,000,000 Indians roaming the country. In 1840 there were about 400,000 of them left. By 1891 there were even fewer. Big Foot's snowy demise was the last act in the Indians' tragic story. Thereafter there was no glorious battles, no great uprisings. The once proud Indians finally capitulated to the whiteman. The wide-open spaces could no longer be called the 'Wild West' - the west was civilised and with it the Indians. This taming was at a terrifically high price and resulted in the loss of an entire culture. The defeat of the Indians had taken less than thirty years, from the first signs of insurrection in Minnesota in 1862. During the executions that followed the Minnesota Massacre, two of the Sioux ringleaders - Shakopee and Medicine Bottle - were hanged at Fort Snelling. As Shakopee was about to be executed a train whistle echoed in the distance. "As the white man comes in", moaned Shakopee, "The Indian goes out." Prophetic words indeed.

Chronology

For reasons of conciseness, I've taken the California Gold Rush of 1848 as year zero for the American Indian Wars. I know there were many conflicts before this period, but this guide isn't primarily concerned with them. For an excellent chronology of the entire time span, see *North American Indian Wars* by Richard H Dillon (Arms and Armour Press, 1983) which covers everything from the Conquistadors to Custer.

1848	Californian Gold Rush
1851	Treaty of Laramie
1853	Treaty with Southern Plains Tribes
1854	Ash Creek Massacre (Mk I)
1855	Ash Creek Massacre (Mk II)
1858	Geronimo attacks Arispe
1861	American Civil War begins
	Cochise involved in 'Bascom Incident'
	General Indian raiding begins, due to lack of troops during Civil War
1862	Minnesota Massacre
	Battle of Apache Pass
1863	Battle of Whitestone Hill
	Mangas Coloradas killed
	Battle of Canyon De Chelly
	Little Crow killed
1864	Battle of Abobe Walls (Mk I)
	Sand Creek Massacre
	Battle of Kildeer Mountain
1865	Civil War ends, Indian Wars begin in earnest
	Battle of River Platte
1866	Fetterman Massacre
	Portugee Phillips' ride
1867	Hayfield Fight
	Wagon Box Fight
	Medicine Lodge Creek peace council
	Hancock's War
1868	Fort Laramie Treaty
	Abandonment of Bozeman forts
	Battle of Beecher's Island
	Battle of Washita River

1871	White Bear, Sitting Bear attack grain train
	White Bear, Sitting Bear and Big Tree arrested (Sitting Bear killed)
1872	Captain Jack's Modoc War begins
	Cochise surrenders
1873	Yellowstone River survey
	General Canby assassinated and Captain Jack hanged
1874	Expedition finds gold in Black Hills.
	Red River War (War on the Staked Plains) begins
	Battle of Adobe Walls (Mk II)
	Attack on Palo Duro Canyon
	Cochise dies in captivity
1875	Quanah surrenders
1876	Battle of Rosebud
	Battle of Little Big Horn
	Battle of Warbonnet Creek
1877	Battle of Wolf Mountain
	Chief Joseph and Nez Perce attempt (and fail) to reach Canada
	Crazy Horse is killed
	Sitting Bull escapes to Canada
1878	White Bear commits suicide in prison
1880	Victorio killed
1881	Sitting Bull surrenders
1886	Geronimo finally surrenders
1889	Ghost Dance Cult comes to prominence
1890	Sitting Bull killed
	Battle of Wounded Knee Creek
1904	Chief Joseph dies
1909	Red Cloud and Geronimo die
1911	Quanah Parker dies

Reference Materials

Books

There have been shelves full of books written over the years relating to the history of the American frontier. The following list makes no claims to be definitive, but all the books listed here have proved useful. They range from the light overview to the weighty tome and all are worth a look.

Custer's Luck by Edgar I Stewart (University of Oklahoma Press 1955) Certainly one of the most famous books on Custer's life and death. Over 40 years since its publication it's still highly readable.

North American Indian Wars by Richard H Dillon (Arms & Armour Press 1983) A great, informative look at all the Indian Wars. Well-illustrated with paintings, maps and photos, this is beautifully put together. Good chronology.

The Old West by Time Life Books (various authors 1973) Especially volumes devoted to 'The Indians', 'The Great Chiefs' and 'The Soldiers.' Top-notch leather-bound series from Time Life, these are among the best books on their respective subjects. 'The Soldiers' volume is, in my opinion, the best book on the US Army and the Indian Wars ever published - excellent text and a superb collection of paintings and photographs.

North American Indian Chiefs edited by Karl Nagelfell (Tiger Books International 1997) Brief but informative look at 18 leaders, from Hiawatha through to Geronimo. Good info on early chiefs, illustrated with portraits.

American Indian War Chiefs by Jason Hook (Firebird Books 1989 - reprinted by Brockhampton Press 1998) Good biographies of four chiefs - Tecumseh, Crazy Horse, Chief Joseph and Geronimo. Very well researched, good maps, good chronologies.

The Life History Of The United States (Time Life Books 1963) Another very good series from Time Life, this one spanning the entire history of North America. The following volumes are especially useful: **Vol 4 The Sweep Westward (1829-49), Vol 5 The Union Sundered (1849-65), Vol 6 The Union Restored (1861-76), Vol 7 Steel And Steam (1877-1890).**

The Mammoth Book Of The West by Jon E Lewis (Robinson Publishing 1996) Good introduction to the history of the West, this covers everything from the cattle empires and outlaws to gold rushes and Indians. Readable.

Scalp Dance - Indian Warfare On The High Plains 1865-1879 by Thomas Goodrich (Stackpole Books 1997) An incredible collection of diaries from the period, this is one of the most interesting books on the subject. The information Goodrich has assembled sheds new light on the conditions out West, with vivid accounts of life on the campaign trail, the ferocity of the battles, accounts of Indian and white atrocities, and tales of settlers captured by hostiles.

Bluecoats And Redskins - The United States Army And The Indian 1866-1891 by Robert M Utley (Cassell & Company 1973) Well-researched, detailed analysis of all the post-Civil War conflicts with comprehensive maps and some illustrations. Descriptions of actual battles a little flat, but great in all other departments.

War Cries On Horseback - The History Of The Indian Wars by Steven Longstreet (Sphere Books 1970) Very interesting, though often historically inaccurate, account of the Indian Wars. High on zest and atmosphere, low on social comment.

Once They Moved Like The Wind - Cochise, Geronimo And The Apache Wars by David Roberts (Simon and Schuster 1994 - printed in UK by Pimlico 1998)

Geronimo - The Man, His Time, His Place by Angie Debo (University of Oklahoma Press, 1976 - printed in UK by Pimlico 1993)

The Lance And The Shield - The Life And Times Of Sitting Bull by Robert M Utley (Henry Holt and company 1993 - printed in the UK by Pimlico 1998)

Pimlico have gained a reputation for quality on American historical subjects. These three books are all worth a look, especially Utley's Sitting Bull biography.

History And Military Affairs Volume III: The Nineteenth Century (1967) Interesting perspectives on tactics and achievements of Indian Wars.

Touch The Earth - A Self-portrait of Indian Existence compiled by T C McLuhan (Abacus 1973) A collection of observations from the Indians' point of view, concerning their treatment by the whites. Simple, yet undeniably powerful.

Bury My Heart At Wounded Knee by Dee Brown (Barrie & Jenkins 1971 - reprinted incessantly) Justly famous best-seller that tells the story of the West from the Indians' perspective. Less 'How The West Was Won', but rather 'How Our Heritage Was Lost.' Confusingly punctuated with an Indian-style calendar ("It was the Moon When Geese Lay Eggs" - better known as April), but still the best of its type and an eye-opening contrast with other books of the period (written from the white perspective). Brown has also written other books on the West, including **The Fetterman Massacre (Barrie & Jenkins 1972)**.

Woodenleg - A Warrior Who Fought Custer interpreted by Thomas B Marquis (Midwestern Company 1931) The story of the Battle of the Little Big Horn as told by a participant.

My Life On The Plains Or Personal Experiences With Indians by General George A Custer (University of Oklahoma 1962) An account of Custer's early experiences on the plains, terminating with his service in Kansas in 1868. The last paragraph is particularly ominous, with Custer saying that as he writes these final lines he's looking forward to his next mission - 'an important exploring expedition' in North Dakota - which will set the next part of Custer's career in motion.

North Against The Sioux by Kenneth Ulyatt (Collins 1965) A great little book dramatising the events around Fort Phil Kearny, and concentrating on the story of Portugee Phillips' epic ride for help.

The Nez Perce Indian War by Theodore Mathieson (Monarch 1964) Similar to the above, but dealing with the exploits of Chief Joseph.

Geronimo - His Own Story edited by S M Barrett (New York 1906) Geronimo's life story as told in captivity during 1905-6 to Ace Duklugie (the son of Juh, one of Geronimo's comrades-in-arms during the Apache Wars), who in turn translated it for Barrett.

Captured By Indians - 15 Firsthand Accounts 1750-1870 edited by Fredrick Drimmer (Dover Publications 1951) Exactly what you'd expect from the title, including one very interesting account of life among the Comanches.

The Sacred Pipe - Black Elk's Account Of The Seven Rites Of The Oglala Sioux (University of Oklahoma Press 1953) Including a full description of the wiwanyag wachipi (the Sun Dance), though unsurprisingly no mention of the Ghost Dance.

Documentaries

In addition to these books, there are several excellent documentaries dealing with the West, many of which have been screened on TV. Look out for *The West*, the best of the bunch (especially the episode dealing with the Civil War years entitled 'Death Runs Riot'), *The Wild West* and a one-off documentary entitled *Death Of A Wagon Train* (about the fate of the Donner Party). It's worth seeing some of the programmes screened on the History and Biography Channels (dealing with Custer, Sitting Bull, Geronimo etc). There are also various videos available in the UK and the US, including the series *The Real West* (with voice-over by Kenny Rogers). For those wanting to recreate the frontier atmosphere more realistically, there's a CD available called *Custer's Last Band*, an album of 7th Cavalry music composed by Felix Vinatieri, Custer's legendary bandmaster. The authentic sound is replicated using 'period instruments, including Vinatieri's own E-flat cornet.'

Websites

Nothing on the web is a patch on the books mentioned above for pure scope, depth and detail, with one big exception:

http://www.garryowen.com George A Custer's Homepage. The most impressive site on the Internet dealing with Custer, this is very well put together and crammed with biographical facts, links and opinions. Hugely interesting to anyone beguiled by the Custer myth. It's also got a range of profiles on renowned Custer experts, including Fred Dustin, Earl Alonzo Brininstool, Walter M Camp and Charles Kuhlan (author of 'Legend Into History', widely believed to be the most comprehensive and definitive version of the Battle of the Little Big Horn). On this site you can even donate money to the Custer Battlefield Historical and Museum Association. A must for Custer Buffs (or lovers of 'Custeriana' as it's known). Plenty of links to other aspects of the Indian Wars make this the best site on the web for the subjects covered in this book.

http://www.midastours.co.uk Alternatively you can visit the historic battle sites and locations mentioned in this Pocket Essential by embarking on a 10-day tour entitled 'Custer, The Indian Wars And The Wild West.' Included are visits to Fort Phil Kearny, Wounded Knee, Deadwood and the Black Hills, with a whole day devoted to the Little Big Horn battle site.

There are many sites devoted to Native American Indian culture and history, while **www.amazon.co.uk** has a comprehensive list of Indian Wars material, including many books and videos.

The Essential Library

Build up your library with new titles every month

Film Directors:

Jane Campion (£2.99)	**John Carpenter** (£3.99)
Jackie Chan (£2.99)	**Joel & Ethan Coen** (£3.99)
David Cronenberg (£3.99)	**Terry Gilliam** (£2.99)
Alfred Hitchcock (£3.99)	**Krzysztof Kieslowski** (£2.99)
Stanley Kubrick (£2.99)	**Sergio Leone** (£3.99)
David Lynch (£3.99)	**Brian De Palma** (£2.99)
Sam Peckinpah (£2.99)	**Ridley Scott** (£3.99)
Orson Welles (£2.99)	**Billy Wilder** (£3.99)
Steven Spielberg (£3.99)	

Film Genres:

Film Noir (£3.99)	**Hong Kong Heroic Bloodshed** (£2.99)
Horror Films (£3.99)	**Slasher Movies**(£3.99)
Spaghetti Westerns (£3.99)	**Vampire Films** (£2.99)
Blaxploitation Films (£3.99)	

Film Subjects:

Laurel & Hardy (£3.99)	**Marx Brothers** (£3.99)
Steve McQueen (£2.99)	**Marilyn Monroe** (£3.99)
The Oscars® (£3.99)	**Filming On A Microbudget** (£3.99)
Bruce Lee (£3.99)	

TV:

Doctor Who (£3.99)

Literature:

Cyberpunk (£3.99)	**Philip K Dick** (£3.99)
Hitchhiker's Guide (£3.99)	**Noir Fiction** (£2.99)
Terry Pratchett (£3.99)	**Sherlock Holmes** (£3.99)

Ideas:

Conspiracy Theories (£3.99)	**Nietzsche** (£3.99)
Feminism (£3.99)	

History:

Alchemy & Alchemists (£3.99)	**The Crusades** (£3.99)

Available at all good bookstores, or send a cheque to: **Pocket Essentials (Dept IW), 18 Coleswood Rd, Harpenden, Herts, AL5 1EQ, UK.** Please make cheques payable to 'Oldcastle Books.' Add 50p postage & packing for each book in the UK and £1 elsewhere.

US customers can send $6.95 plus $1.95 postage & packing for each book to: **Trafalgar Square Publishing, PO Box 257, Howe Hill Road, North Pomfret, Vermont 05053, USA.** e-mail: tsquare@sover.net

Customers worldwide can order online at **www.pocketessentials.com**.

The Essential Library

Build up your library with new titles every month

Tim Burton by Colin Odell & Michelle Le Blanc, £3.99

Tim Burton makes films about outsiders on the periphery of society. His heroes are psychologically scarred, perpetually naive and childlike, misunderstood or unintentionally disruptive. They upset convential society and morality. Even his villains are rarely without merit - circumstance blurs the divide between moral fortitude and personal action. But most of all, his films have an aura of the fairytale, the fantastical and the magical.

Film Music by Paul Tonks, £3.99

From *Ben-Hur* to *Star Wars* and *Psycho* to *Scream*, film music has played an essential role in such genre-defining classics. Making us laugh, cry, and jump with fright, it's the manipulative tool directors cannot do without. The turbulent history, the ever-changing craft, the reclusive or limelight-loving superstars, the enthusiastic world of fandom surrounding it, and the best way to build a collection, is all streamlined into a user-friendly guide for buffs and novices alike.

Woody Allen (Revised & Updated Edition) by Martin Fitzgerald, £3.99

Woody Allen: Neurotic. Jewish. Funny. Inept. Loser. A man with problems. Or so you would think from the characters he plays in his movies. But hold on. Allen has written and directed 30 films. He may be a funny man, but he is also one of the most serious American film-makers of his generation. This revised and updated edition includes *Sweet And Lowdown* and *Small Time Crooks*.

American Civil War by Phil Davies, £3.99

The American Civil War, fought between North and South in the years 1861-1865, was the bloodiest and most traumatic war in American history. Rival visions of the future of the United States faced one another across the battlefields and, as in any civil war, families and friends were bitterly divided by the conflict. Phil Davies looks at the deep-rooted causes of the war, so much more complicated than the simple issue of slavery.

American Indian Wars by Howard Hughes, £3.99

At the beginning of the 1840s the proud tribes of the North American Indians looked across the plains at the seemingly unstoppable expansion of the white man's West. During the decades of conflict that followed, as the new world pushed onward, the Indians saw their way of life disappear before their eyes. Over the next 40 years they clung to a dream of freedom and a continuation of their traditions, a dream that was repeatedly shattered by the whites.

Available at all good bookstores, or send a cheque to: **Pocket Essentials (Dept IW), 18 Coleswood Rd, Harpenden, Herts, AL5 1EQ, UK**. Please make cheques payable to 'Oldcastle Books.' Add 50p postage & packing for each book in the UK and £1 elsewhere.

US customers can send $6.95 plus $1.95 postage & packing for each book to: **Trafalgar Square Publishing, PO Box 257, Howe Hill Road, North Pomfret, Vermont 05053, USA**. e-mail: tsquare@sover.net

Customers worldwide can order online at **www.pocketessentials.com**.